Discover the thrill of learning to sail.

Celebrate the joy and freedom of Barbara's sailing adventures with sail master Sam.

You will tune into the natural world by sharing the intricate skills of reading the weather and the ever changing patterns of the sea.

Appreciate the challenges of learning to sail as they explore together the stunning coastal waters of south western Cyprus on Toppers, a Hobie Wave and a Hobie 15 catamaran.

This is a journey of breaking through personal barriers as they evolve from teacher and student towards becoming an experienced sailing team.

SAILING WITH SAM

BARBARA JONES

Published by Reids House Publishing

© 2015 Reids House Publishing. All rights reserved.

Cover photograph © 2012 Barbara Jones

ISBN 978-9963-2184-1-7

DEDICATION

With deep gratitude for the inspiration
of the sailors past, present and future,
who smell the salty sea,
and dare to sail.

ACKNOWLEDGEMENTS

With thanks and appreciation to Sam Thompson (known as Tomo by UK friends), for his hard work and *im*patience when teaching me to sail (it truly worked wonders), and for his *dis*belief that this book would ever come to fruition, which pushed me forward to prove otherwise. Our deepening relationship has been one of the greatest gifts of this experience.

A very big thank you to Dianne Ward, my gifted editor and long standing friend, for demanding of me my best to bring to life my love of sailing. My Technical Advisor, Phil Mutton, Training Officer at the Paphos International Sailing Club (PISC), Cyprus used his skills as a highly experienced sailor and RYA Dinghy Senior Instructor to comb through the details and untangle the knots for a smooth passage. Many thanks Phil.

The Royal Yacht Association (RYA) have been helpful throughout. I would like to thank them for the wonderful training books they have available for beginner sailors. Most helpful to me as a novice sailor has been RYA GO SAILING! – and its companion book RYA GO SAILING! Activity book. I highly recommend these for beginners of any age.

I wish to express my appreciation to Frank de Marko, Brian Snellgrove and Françoise Sauze, Francesca Pinoni and Rachael Petrou; for giving me valuable feedback during the writing process.

CONTENTS

Introduction

"Why learn to sail?" I frequently asked myself in 2012. I have always loved water; the way it wraps itself around you, supports you and even rocks you gently as the waves roll in an out. It can also tease and taunt you, leaving you beaten, bruised and exhausted. As an avid swimmer, I hold water in deep respect. It can be fast and furious or as soft as a glistening mirror that you can skim across, changing within hours on the same day.

I paddled Canadian C1 (one paddler) and C2 (2 paddlers) canoes competitively when I was in my twenties. I had trained in the Adirondacks, USA and had quickly gained notoriety as it was quite an unusual sport for a young woman. I loved the sport; the rhythm of the paddle, the swoosh of the bow cutting through the water, the complex body movements required for steering and the deep sense of satisfaction as I became one with the boat.

While I was living in the seaside town of Morecambe my bank ran an incentive to support new outdoor activities. Knowing my interest in water sports, I was approached and offered an interest-free extended loan to purchase a windsurfer and any other support equipment I would need. I jumped at the opportunity and bought a Thor (which at 18 kg was one of the lightest around at the time), a car roof rack with runners that I could slide the board onto, boots and gloves. The bank only required regular repayments, updates, photos and for me to keep the windsurfer for a minimum of three years.

I was teaching at the time. During the weeks of high tide I dashed home with my windsurfer on top of my car, changed into my wetsuit and was out again on and my way to the sea within 15 minutes. One of my neighbors enjoyed timing me, giving me thumbs up when I bettered my best time. Morecambe Bay is deep, with the town of Morecambe on one side and Barrow in Furness on the other. The running tide pours in at high tide and leaves huge expanses of sand at low tide. There were some seasonal changes but the winds appeared to be directly related to this in-pouring and outpouring. When you knew the tidal movement, you knew the wind direction. From my experience back then, I arrogantly believed that I had a good sense of wind direction and sailing skills. That was until I really began to sail!

I moved to Pissouri in Cyprus in 1994. Cyprus is an island in the Mediterranean very close to the Turkish mainland, Israel and Libya. Presently the island is split into the northern Turkish Cypriot side and the southern Greek Cypriot side. There are two main mountain ranges the Girne range in the north and the Troodos range in the south.

Pissouri is a small village nestled in the folds of the foothills overlooking the sea on the Greek side. Directly behind Pissouri to the north sits the Troodos Mountain range leading up to Mt Olympus its highest point at over 1,800ft. Pissouri is linked to the main towns: Limassol (45km away), Paphos (35km away) and Larnaca (110km away) as well as the one and only city Nicosia (140km away), by a reasonably well maintained highway which makes travelling the island very easy.

In December 2011, I met Sam. Sam had spent the summer of 2011 sailing a Hobie Wave Catamaran in the nearby town of Paphos. He had owned speedboats in the U.K. but enjoyed sailing a catamaran so much that he bought a Hobie 15 Club, a superfast sport catamaran that he kept in Limassol. Sam is a self taught sailor with a highly tuned perception of wind strength, speed and direction developed from his days as a farmer's son. His depth of knowledge and experience gave him confidence on the water. Eager to sail Sam invited me to join him for our first sail together.

The adventure begins.

Inaugural Sail with Sam

Tuesday May 8th

We arrived at West Wind Water Sports Centre, a colourful array of catamarans, canoes and windsurfs poised enticingly on the beach at the "Four Seasons Hotel", Limassol. George, the owner, welcomed us with an enormous smile, eyes twinkling. He introduced me to his paradise with pride offering us both the use of sun beds, canoes and full use of the beach and all the facilities. It was a perfect location, for the little harbor provided mooring space for the jet skis, rescue, ski and dive boats and the shallow lagoon was a perfect place to swim.

We were hot, sticky and dusty from our 40 minute drive from Pissouri, so a cooling dip in the lagoon came first. As I sank into the lapping, cooling waves I stretched catlike, feeling the salt water caress and rock me, then with a burst of energy I swam over to a catamaran moored in the lagoon. Making full use of the momentum I lifted my arms up onto the hull, kicked and pulled myself onto the boat. "Hey, Sam, look!" I called. With my legs dangling in the water and lying across the hull I turned to him with a big smile of success. As I did so I felt a painful click. My lower ribcage spasmed as one of my ribs on the right side popped. It had been pressured by the twist and the unyielding hull and trapped by the buckle on my life jacket. This tore the cartilage. Ouch! It served me right for showing off.

We continued our leisurely swim. I took it very easy floating on my back. Sam swam close by, keeping an eye on me. I had hurt my rib trying to prove I could pull myself up out of the water onto the catamaran in case of emergency. It had been a concern of Sam's and a condition that he had set for us sailing together in case I ever went overboard or if we capsized. Undaunted by the pain, I knew I had technically passed Sam's test.

Sam loved sailing his Hobie Club 15, a catamaran built for racing which is fast and sensitive to handling. He had already experienced a number of capsizes, the most dramatic being a cartwheel, where the stern flips over the **bows**. This, he explained, is caused by the **bows** (at the front of the boat), being submerged by the waves. The bow stops but the **stern** (the back of the boat), which still has momentum, flips up and over. The **helmsman** and **crew** are flung off. His concern was that it can be dangerous as it happens so fast you do not know where you are going to land or what is going to land on top of you. If all is well then the boat has to be **righted** (turned the right way up, back on its hulls), which is a team effort and the helmsman and crew have to be able to clamber back onboard. Although aware of the challenges and dangers I felt I wanted to try to learn to sail. I was determined not to let the injury hold me back. It made me more resolute.

Once we dried off Sam introduced me to his catamaran, "Sam's Kitten Cat". She looked tall and impressive as she sat in the sand amongst the other boats with a **mast** 7.2 meters tall. The **trampoline deck** was laced to the two white fiberglass 4.95 metre long **hulls** and the two cross beams of 2.26 meters. As he showed me around her he demonstrated where we would sit and explained that today my role would be to watch and listen. Sam usually sails solo but today he would be **helmsman** (and steer the boat) and I would be **crew** (assisting in the sail).

The helmsman sits at the stern of the boat close to the two **rudders** (one for each hull) with the **rudder bar** connecting them. In a dinghy it is called the tiller. The direction of the rudders determines the direction of the bow of the boat. He showed me how he used the **rudder extension**, a long pole which he rested on his shoulder. This allows the helmsman more flexibility to control the boat. The crew has to sit further up the hull and move to a position closer to the **fore** (front of the boat) or **aft** (back of the boat) near to the helmsman depending on the sea and the wind conditions. This fore and aft balancing is called **trimming** the boat..

Sam took his sails out of George's sail store and placed them on the deck. I felt my first pang of anxiety as my stomach knotted and my first rigging lesson began. As Sam unrolled the brightly coloured **jib sail** (this is a small sail often called the **foresail**), he showed me how to attach it to the **halyard** which comes down the front of the mast. He deftly attached the sail with a clip onto the *forestays* (long metal wires which keep the mast in place and upright), before hauling the jib sail up. He then handed me a clip to attach to the *clew* (reinforced point at the foot of the jib). There were two bright yellow *sheets* (ropes) attached known as jib sheets. He pulled on one sheet which pulled the fluttering jib sail to the left side of the mast and then the other which pulled the jib sail to the right. He explained that today during our sail he would control these but normally the crew would control the bright yellow jib sheets to switch the side where the jib sail is set according to the wind. Handling the jib sheets helped me enormously as I am dyslexic and usually challenged when working out which is my left and right hand. I had been worried about following directional instructions on our first sail. I breathed a sigh of relief. I really did not want to make a fool of myself. Sam went on to explain that the jib sail is simply called the jib. As the catamaran turns, the jib scoops up the wind first, like a secondary engine turning wheels of a car, enabling the *mainsail* (larger central sail) acting as the main engine, to fill quickly and pick up the speed.

He unrolled the larger *mainsail* and showed me where this sail is attached. The Hobie 15 catamaran does not have a *boom* (a heavy bar attached to the mast and bottom of the sail). Many sailboats do and you have to duck out of the way when you change direction or you can get a sharp bang on the head. Sam demonstrated that his catamaran has a *loose footed sail* (without a boom), but warned me I still have to duck, as it moves across the deck very quickly.

The *mainsheet* (rope) was thick, soft and beautifully textured when I ran it through my fingers. It needs to be soft on the hands as this is the main control for wind speed and is in use almost all the time. It is used to adjust the angle of the sail to the wind and is attached to the *clew* (bottom corner of the sail away from the mast) of the mainsail. Sam turned the mast to show me how it rotated on the *mast foot* (a pivoting joint at the bottom of the mast) and he let me turn it to see how smoothly it rotated from side to side making the mainsail more efficient, so that it can scoop in more wind. He then fixed the top of the sail into a groove in the mast and handed me a rope he called a *halyard* and asked me to hoist the sail. As I pulled on the halyard again and again, the *luff* of the sail slid up the groove in the mast and the sail unfurled.

I gasped as the lovely yellow, white and black sail filled and fluttered in the wind. Sam then let me pull the **downhaul** (a rope at the bottom of the sail next to the mast) as hard as I could. I then looped it once through the **K cleat** (a K shaped hook) on the mast, back up to a clew at the bottom of the sail and then pulling down really tightly fastening off the downhaul making figures of eight around the cleat. As I stood back and admired my efforts I could see that pulling the downhaul very tight makes the sail smooth and taut. The halyard was then secured to the mast. By this time my head was buzzing with all the new terms but I felt I was beginning to grasp the basic principles. I shivered with anticipation as we rolled the catamaran, which was loaded on the beach trailer, down to the water's edge.

Waist deep in the water Sam held on to the catamaran. Holding her steady he told me to jump on, which I did gingerly, gasping as my rib complained. I moved cautiously towards the **bow** (front of the catamaran)) and waited anxiously, uncertain, alone. Was there anything I missed? Perhaps there was something I needed to do? I felt enormously relieved when Sam jumped aboard.

In one swift movement he grasped hold of the tiller extension (which controls the rudders), and the mainsheet. Focusing ahead of us he said he was **turning into the wind.** Gently Sam swept the rudders from side to side as he edged the catamaran forward. It was nerve wracking for me as Sam twitched and adjusted the mainsheet, edging past each boat in the harbour with focused attention, guiding us safely out to sea.

Totally absorbed by the precision and flow of each manoeuvre I jumped, startled when the sails filled with a whooshing, snapping sound. Free of the other boats we shot past the breakwater. We were out at sea! Sam pulled the sail in tight. As we flew across the water everything became a blur. I gripped on tight and closed my eyes to revel in the wind-rush. The salt stung my cheeks. I raised my arms to feel the weightlessness and sheer joy of taking flight across the water.

The faster we sailed the more the hull we were sitting on lifted out of the water. With his hair streaking behind him, Sam grinned, piratanically. With the tiller extension over his shoulder he leaned back, reining in the power of the mainsail with the mainsheet. We were dashing across waves, jostling with the white horses. As we stampeded through the waves I soared, the whistling wind combing and ruffling my hair, salt-splashed, elated.

Sam reached out for the jib sheet and called out, "Ready! Watch and move across quickly. Sit on the other hull when I do". I clung on terrified, uncertain. My rib started to throb intensely. I was unnerved having landed from that flight of sheer joy so abruptly. I was back in the real world. The sails were humming a deep drone and the clips on the halyard chattered hysterically on the mast, demanding attention. As the catamaran turned momentary silence. Sam pulled on the jib sheet and as he brought the rudders round he moved gracefully to the other side. I hurled myself across to the other hull, aware the halyard was chattering once more, grimacing with rib pain. I was thankful to be wearing dive boots because I almost caught my toe in the matting on the trampoline.

We shot forward once more, I was instantly soaked. Torrents of cold water gushed with a loud swoosh over the bow. It felt as if buckets and buckets of water were being thrown with immense strength directly at me as we sliced through the waves. The stinging shock of the cold salty water took my breath away. The deafening wind and sheer terror of the speed at which we travelled started to chill me to the core. I fought against the cold, clamping down on my chattering teeth which did not help to relieve the dull ache of the rib. Sam turned and grinned. My discomfort diminished. I began to feel the exhilaration of riding the waves and the wind once more. As the sails began to hum they seemed to celebrate our companionship and the triumph of a challenge shared and conquered.

We turned and turned again and again, as we continued our sail. After an hour, we returned exhausted and elated.

At the end of the day my brain felt quite overloaded with all the information I had taken in. I felt physically exhausted, probably from pent-up tension built up through the readiness to act on instructions. However, I realized that thinking and doing are quite different processes. I felt hopeful that with more opportunities to sail processing and remembering the instructions would become easier. I laughed as I realized that this was a perfect opportunity to make full use of all five senses, the perfect mode of learning for dyslexics. Perhaps this is what the term "sensible" really means.

My Second Sail!

Tuesday May 15th

It was a warmer day and cosseted in my thermal T-shirt I was feeling better prepared than previously and eager to sail. My rib was still hurting, stabbing pains radiated from the sternum when I turned or twisted suddenly making me catch my breath. However, I was determined to prove to Sam that I could tolerate the inevitable bumps and bruises of sailing.

I had survived two major car accidents, one in 1984 and one in 1998. It was my determination not to become a victim and limit my life that enabled me to discover the Feldenkrais Method®. This was developed by Moshe Feldenkrais, a top Israeli scientist, engineer and Judo expert. I left my teaching career in Cairo at its peak, as a result of the first accident, to become a Feldenkrais Practitioner in order to help people with pain management, movement co-ordination and balance issues. Having completed my 4 years of training as a practitioner in 1994, the second accident gave me the opportunity to put all I had learnt into practice for myself. Pain was no stranger but I had insider knowledge of how we can retrain ourselves to not only recover but move even better than before. Learning to slow down and be more precise in movement enabled me to fine tune myself to the point where I moved better after my recovery than I had ever done before.

I appreciate and greatly value the opportunity to learn to sail with Sam. I had certainly not been put off by the soaking and the speed. Far from it! I had found it exhilarating and could not wait to be out on the water once more. I knew today's sailing would be extremely wet and fast as Sam wanted to sail for longer and to sail further.

As Sam manoeuvred "Sam's Kitten Cat" past the yachts and dinghies moored in the lagoon, I watched in earnest rather than with the trepidation of the week before. I was fascinated and eager to learn how he managed to manoeuvre the boat so effortlessly and I yearned to be able to do the same. I watched his every move with the eyes of a novice sailor but the skill of the scientific and engineering knowledge of a Feldenkrais Practitioner. Feldenkrais Practitioners love to ask the question, "How do I do what I do and how can I make it easier, more comfortable and with that, graceful?" As Sam tweaked the mainsail and jib effortlessly I watched him smoothly navigate as he moved the rudders back and forth.

Once in the open sea, the sails caught the wind immediately. They seemed to hum and looked taut and shiny as the mast snapped around to maximize the scooping up of the wind in the sails. As we sped across the waves I could feel my body tense and my rib start to throb once more. Relax, relax I told myself. As I listened attentively to Sam's instructions as we *came about* (turned the catamaran's bows through the wind), I realized I was using too much effort and hurling myself across the boat. I was being driven by the panic of the moment. I had not yet grasped that this was a controlled manoeuvre which would happen time and time again when sailing. Sam suggested that I take it slowly and crawl catlike across the trampoline deck. Not only was this more comfortable but I could watch what he was doing at the same time.

I was intrigued by the movement of the tiller bar which connected the two rudders. When he moved the bar towards him the bows of the catamaran moved in the opposite direction to his hand movement. In order to make use of the tiller bar only, he tossed the tiller extension off the boat into the sea (whilst still attached to the bar of course) and then retrieved it after the manoeuvre and placed it back on his shoulder once more. I felt a surge of panic; surely I would get the tiller extension tangled up in the rigging at the first opportunity. The moment I had that thought Sam waved to me to change places and handed over the helm position to me.

Anxiously I put the extension bar on my shoulder where it needed to stay balanced so that I could feel the tug of the rudders through the pole. Sam was right about the tug. I could feel the rudders pulling and straining, wanting to go with the flow of the sea but being forced to follow my direction. Maintaining a course required an enormous amount of strength, determination and concentration. My wounded rib fought me all the way. With the tiller extension in my left hand, all the effort seemed to be focused on the right rib. It felt like a drill penetrating bone and tissue. It began to screech out to me with deep intense pain but I hung in there.

With me acting as helmsman Sam took over as crew and worked the jib sheets, guiding me through my first turn. His instruction was to throw the tiller extension over the stern of the boat and duck out of the way of the sail as I manoeuvred the rudders with the tiller bar. In order to *tack* (turn the bow of the boat through the wind passing through the "no-go zone"), I was to push the tiller bar away from me and to watch out when the sail flipped across. I had to loosen off the sail just a little, duck and get on the other side of the catamaran. From there I needed to be ready to aim her at the next *point of sail* (a landmark or particular spot to direct the boat towards) with my hand on the rudder bar, then lean out and collect the rudder extension again. As I followed through the first manoeuvre and leaned out to pull in the rudder extension my ribs screeched reaching a new level of pain. My first attempt was far from perfect. I gritted my teeth and tried again.

Strangely enough, the pain kept me focused. I was able to banish the overwhelming chattering thoughts and instead tried to break the process down. I asked myself questions about which way to pull the rudder bar, towards me or away, then immediately felt the effects that it had on which way the bow of the boat would turn. Once I gave myself the opportunity to feel it and sense it I got better and better and the pain sat sulkily in the background.

It had been a challenging day. There had been so much to learn but I felt elated by the sense of achievement. I was beginning to realize that sailing is a continuing learning spiral and not something you learn in a few weeks. My greatest achievement had been that despite the pain I had not given up. But above all I loved the speed and the feeling of weightlessness, not just in the physical sense but for a whole day all of my worries and cares had simply been blown away.

A Fabulous Day!

Tuesday June 5rd

As we set sail the sun beamed down on my olive oil saturated skin. The smell of this elixir used by the ancient Greek Olympiads shields my sensitive fair skin from the sun's rays and protects me from burns. With my spirits high I feel more secure and self-confident, ready for what the day will bring.

Sam had set the objective of sailing across Limassol Bay towards the harbour. This was the first of our destination sails. Along the coastline the beaches had been improved and protected by the breakwaters built a quarter of a mile out to sea. This encouraged the sand that sweeps in towards the beaches to collect and form shallower swimming areas. The shallows have softer, less turbulent waters, creating warm, safer water for swimming. Beyond the breakwaters the riotous waves (wild, cold and uninviting) pound against the man made barriers.

Tempted to enjoy an easy sail Sam slid the catamaran in through a gap between two of the breakwaters. It felt as if we were sailing on an inland waterway rather than the sea. As we were in close proximity to the land, we could clearly see people on the beaches, having barbeques and playing beach tennis and volley ball. As we skimmed along, enthusiastic swimmers waved and swam out to us. Enjoying our reception, we followed the line of breakwaters all along the Limassol coast right up to the old harbor. Just before we reached the harbor we slipped through the last gap in the breakwaters and we were back out to sea once more yet within easy reach of the harbour.

The water was choppy and the wind challenging us to fly once more. Sam encouraged me to take the helm. My rib was still painful, resisting the reaching and pulling actions essential to sailing but the pain was manageable only flaring a warning during quick or over hasty movements. Watching me carefully, Sam spotted a couple of my covert grimaces and took over the helm. Once we had reached the old Limassol Harbor, as we began to *tack* back. *Tack* is an economical sailing term as it has a number of meanings depending on what you are actually doing at the time. Here, it refers to the zigzag sailing pattern often needed in order to sail from point A to point B and make the most of the wind. I took the helm for short spells. It had been a wonderful sail within the breakwater; gloriously peaceful with the gentle waves simply drawing us along. It was the first time we were close enough to the land to see people waving, smiling and swimming out to us: watching us sail was making people happy. This planted a seed deep within me. I felt a deep desire to find a way to share these moments. Sam turned to me and smiled, it was our longest sail from a point A to point B yet. Sailing with Sam was beginning to mean a lot more to me than I had anticipated. These shared moments were deepening our appreciation of each other.

We were enjoying the moment. Glowing with the success of sailing across Limassol Bay from the Four Seasons Hotel to the old harbor and the warm welcomes we received, we were feeling blissful about an easy uneventful sail. With the sails humming, a sign they were perfectly aligned and the catamaran perfectly trimmed and balanced we started our return journey.

The wind was perfect. We were racing along and had just turned to give each other a big grin when we heard a sharp, shrill sound behind us. It was a life guard hurtling towards us on his bright red jet ski, frantically blowing his whistle and waving. We waved back at him in a friendly manner as he continued racing towards us. Once within earshot, scarlet faced, he screamed at us to stop. He then began to berate us for having sailed inside the breakwater system. He screamed at us over the wind, we had broken the law and he had called the police.

We were astonished. As far as we were aware, motorized boats were quite rightly banned from the swimming area for safety reasons but not windsurfers and small sail boats. Everyone we had met had been so friendly and delighted to see us, except it turned out, one lady. She had rushed off to report our misdemeanor resulting in the appearance of this apoplectic life guard. It was obvious to us that he was angrier at the fact that we had not stopped immediately when we heard his whistle than anything else. He had assumed that we had been "running away" from him and so now self righteously he believed he had "caught us up". Little did he realize that the humming of the sails and buzzing of the shrouds can be quite deafening. We had barely been aware of him even when he was close behind us. Besides that, If we had tried to "run away" he would not have been able to catch us, as our potential for accessing wind speed was far greater than his little jet ski's performance. In reality we had tampered with his sense of importance.

Once he realized we were not going to argue with him and that in fact we were quite stunned, bemused he left. Our day in tatters, we sat and decided what to do. We could go back directly and deal with the wrath of the local police force and risk the night in jail that the life guard had threatened us with, or we could carry on sailing and deal with it later.

We decided to rescue the day and went on to have a glorious sail. How happy we were that we did.

An amused George was waiting for us on our return. We were sailing one of his catamarans, which was obvious from the sail number. He had been phoned by the police. They had informed him of the complaint. They were most apologetic, as they had assumed we were tourists who probably did not know of the local regulations. George assured them that we would not make a habit of sailing inside the breakwater and that we were not too upset with the lifeguard. We breathed a deep sigh of relief.

In retrospect we both had much to learn about the rules, regulations and formalities for Cyprus coastal waters. In addition, I felt a sense of achievement in that today, with Sam, a common goal had been achieved. Together we had dealt diplomatically with a rather officious lifeguard and mutually basked in the pleasure of achieving a near perfect sail.

Tiller Tantrums

Tuesday July 10th

Sailing practice is becoming more comfortable because of the warming wind and water. The air temperature is around about 28 degrees daily. Not only is the sea warming up but the warmer air encourages our clothes and skin to dry faster, but I still got very, very wet.

I was beginning to grasp the differences between tacking (you turn the bow of the boat through the "no-go zone" of the funnel of direct wind) and gybing (turning the stern through the "no-go zone" of the funnel of direct wind). There is very little direct line sailing, most of the time we had to sail in a zigzag pattern to avoid the "windless" area directly into the wind funnel. Correct use of the tiller is essential for turning the boat in the desired direction. However, I still felt clumsy and awkward throwing the tiller extension over the back of the boat, whilst at the same time grabbing hold of the tiller bar. It was not simply the co-ordination of the action but mental resistance to throwing something overboard followed by the worry of retrieving it. It became an obsession exacerbated by failure and fueled by my frustration. With failed turn after failed turn the pressure became so intense I wanted to stamp my feet and scream. Sam had assured me over and over again that this was the best method to begin with; otherwise the tiller extension could get caught up in the **mainsheet,** resulting in instant capsizing. The secret, Sam confided, was to make one fluid movement whilst keeping my eye on the point of sail after I had ducked out of the way of the mainsheet. I learnt through my errors but it was a tough way to learn! The sail moves across very fast. I would be focusing on retrieving the tiller extension when the mainsheet would swing round and catch my neck, face or chin. It really hurt. In fact a couple of times I actually saw stars! Not only was I failing to turn the catamaran, I was getting bumps on my head, bruises on my face and whiplash to my neck. Could it actually get any worse I thought desperately? Sam was at a loss, he could not understand why I could not get what to him was a simple, essential navigational manoeuvre. There were moments when I would have happily jumped off the boat and swam for it.

Having finally completed a successful manoeuvre and set the next *point of sail* (the direction to sail towards) by looking down the windward hull, as the helm I had to plot the next maneuver and, when ready, prepare the crew. It makes a big difference if you are tacking or gybing. Tacking tends to be gentler with less risk of capsizing as you are sailing *upwind* (towards the wind) which is more stable. The helm changes the direction of the boat by turning the bow through the wind or the "no-go zone". When gybing you are sailing *downwind* (with the wind behind you virtually pushing the boat) as the stern of the boat is turned through the wind. This is much less stable.

Having achieved some level of success it was time to return. As Sam took the helm I had time to reflect. I recognized that today I had reached levels of frustration and anger with myself that had almost got to the point of self sabotage. I had gone beyond listening, beyond understanding, simply diving deeper and deeper into a well of self doubt. I eventually broke through that barrier when I gathered myself together and listened to Sam explaining in the simplest terms that the tiller extension can stay in the water indefinitely, as long as I keep my hand on the rudder bar and therefore remain in control of the rudders.

Flotilla Expansion

Tuesday July 17th

Although we loved sailing the Hobie 15, Sam had been hankering for a Hobie Wave to add to his personal flotilla. He had begun his sailing experience on a Wave. He had enthused about how they were steady reliable boats, difficult to capsize and an easy craft on which to learn skills.

Intrigued and eager to gain sailing experience, I began to search the internet and eventually found a Hobie Wave on Bazaraki, a Cyprus based e-shopping site. I found it in early May and mentioned it to Sam a couple of times however at the time he was busy with the finalization of his business affairs in the UK. Undeterred, I contacted the seller, myself. He was an active member of the Farmagusta Sailing Club. He was eager to sell the Wave and free up boat space at the club. In addition he offered a couple of Toppers, little solo sail boats as a free incentive. At that point Sam became very interested and was keen to learn more!

We decided to drive up to Proteras, about 180 km away, to look at the boats. Arriving in Proteras, we had some difficulty finding the Famagusta Sailing Club and phoned the seller. He offered to meet us near a central roundabout in Proteras so that he could guide us to the sailing club. The club, it turned out was tucked away down a series of country roads. We would never have found it without his help.

The Hobie Wave, a 13 ft catamaran, "Kitty Maran," looked rather sad and dejected. It was obvious she had not been sailed for a long time. The seller explained he had been very busy and had not been able to prioritize sailing. He took us to look at the Toppers which at first glance looked like children's play boats, one blue and one red, their hulls paled through sun damage. The seller had bought them second hand some time before hoping that his son's would share his interest in sailing. I could not imagine sailing one myself but could see them as possible learner boats for youngsters.

Sam agreed to the purchase on condition a road trailer capable of transporting all three boats was found. Within a few days the seller called us with the good news. He had located a second hand well used trailer. We drove to Proteras and this time found the Famagusta Sailing.

The boats were already loaded onto the trailer. The condition of the trailer, however, was way below our expectations. Having been asked to pay €350 we'd hoped for a trailer fit for our needs. I felt quite outraged and was quite prepared for Sam to refuse to take the boats, particularly when we learnt the trailer was owned by a high ranking member of the club. The Wave by itself is a heavy boat and with the added weight of two Toppers it looked as if it would barely make it up the road. Even to my inexperienced eye I could see that it was heavily corroded, quite rotten in places and that its wheels simply did not look right. They were askew, very rusty and battered.

Tight jawed, Sam attached the trailer to his Suzuki jeep. It wobbled on its two wheels behind us, even though we took it very slowly. Eventually we stopped and had to make a risk assessment. If we were going to go on the highway we may risk losing something from the trailer but we would have a clear, almost traffic-free, journey. If we take the old B road it may be safer, in that we could keep stopping along the way, but it would be a much longer journey and we would fry in the summer heat. The temperature was the deciding factor. It was hot, really, really searing and still early in the day.

Sam decided to go carefully on the highway, accepting there could be a problem, but he hoped that through careful monitoring, we could keep difficulties to a minimum. The only air conditioning in Sam's Suzuki jeep is the flow of air and breeze through the windows and open top but we also had the glare of the sun to contend with. Driving slowly and carefully we were soon cooking. Sam sat there straight-backed and tight-jawed in a prickly cocoon of silence, monitoring every shifting sound and vibration. I felt completely shut out. Not wanting to increase his stress level I looked furtively over my shoulder every time I heard a squeak. The rest of the time I had my eyes riveted on the passenger wing mirror ready to alert him if anything slipped or moved about on the trailer, but dreading having to do so. As the scorching heat burned in through the open windows my heart was thumping so hard with anxiety I was sure Sam could be hear it.

When, finally, we pulled up outside Sam's apartment in Pissouri, I stepped out of the jeep stiffly and untangled my tension-riddled joints, exhausted. It was only then that Sam told me that with over 30 kilometers to go, the bearings of one of the wheels had completely disintegrated. From that point we could have lost the trailer and boats at any time. The stress for Sam had been enormous as he could feel every shifting vibration of the trailer through his steering wheel and hear the moment to moment changes in resonance during the whole journey back. However, he had decided that it was safer to keep on moving, hence his silence. I was horrified. No wonder my heart had been thumping!

Still in shock but greatly relieved to have arrived safely I helped Sam unpack the Toppers. We put the hulls in his car parking area and took the sails, masts and all the boxes of bits inside. The boxes held a treasure trove which we spread out on the floor in his apartment. There were an assortment of **tell tails**, red and green fluttery ribbons which stick onto the sails as wind guides so the instructions said. There were masses of spare parts including a bailer and bailer chute, coils of rope in different colours, thicknesses and stages of wear and tear as well as clips, rollers, cleats for holding and securing ropes and pulleys for ropes of various sizes. In my minds-eye all the boat parts began to merge and I could see the sail boats begin to emerge. There were other, less easy to identify parts which we assumed must belong to the Toppers, as part of their rigging. However, we had no rigging instructions, not even pictures so to begin with it was all guess work.

Neither boat had been used for many years. The seller had had no idea of their age. They had simply gathered dust and sun damage, forgotten and unloved. They have molded plastic hulls. "Vitamin C" had been red which has faded to a dusky pale rose pink. "Blue Tac" had been a bright vibrant blue was now a light, mottled, pale sky blue. The sails were the original Topper red, white and blue. Even though both boats were rather faded through sun damage, upon close examining the hulls both looked water tight.

Eager to get the boats on the water I offered to explore the internet for information and rigging instructions. By the end of the day I had printed off a wonderful little rigging booklet. I felt very proud of myself when I presented it to a delighted Sam. He had not been expecting such immediate results. Sam had been planning to spend a week or two week tinkering about on his own. Instead we began this, our first shared project, right away. Together we listed and checked the parts in duplicate for each boat. Satisfied that they all seemed to be there, the next challenge was to rig and sail them.

It had been a harrowing adventure which could have gone badly wrong. On the journey from Proteras, during the silence, I had been filled with guilt, convinced that we were in danger of a road accident through my selfish enthusiasm to expand my sailing experience. Thankfully the excitement of the new project carried us both forward and onwards towards a new level of team work.

First Sail in Pissouri Bay

Thursday July 19th

With great trepidation I helped Sam load up the jeep with the sails and equipment. Sam hooked on the temporarily-repaired trailer, sporting a second hand replacement wheel. The trailer was already loaded with the Toppers and off we went.

Each boat had to be carried down to the water's edge. We started with Vitamin C, I held the *painter*, (the front tie or "grab-handle") and Sam held the back. The hulls were much heavier than we had anticipated. Luckily he has very strong fingers as there is only a narrow ledge to grip. We slithered and side stepped over the stones on Pissouri's rocky beach. We took her down the shale slope close to the water's edge and then brought Blue Tac. The two boats sat side by side, as comfortable as old friends, with the water lapping around them. We then brought down the rigging, and as described by the booklet laid each piece beside each boat.

Toppers were designed as trainer boats, particularly favoured by sailing clubs as they are light to carry and transport (they say) on the roof of a car and easy for youngsters to "right" when they capsize.

I had crewed for a friend on Lake Windermere in the English Lake District many years before. Many years later, whilst I was in New York for my Feldenkrais Training I helped out at weekends as an extra hand on boats run by a charity for handicapped adults who wanted to sail. I had even sailed a Topper whilst holidaying in Sharm El Sheikh when I live in Egypt. My memory of the experience was faint. It must have been washed away by all the water I swallowed! I spent more time in the water than sailing as I had to right it several times. Although Sam had had plenty of experience with speed boats and catamarans, sailing dinghies was to be a new experience for him, too. Neither of us had ever even rigged a dinghy.

With the rigging booklet in hand we began our first full rigging practice on Blue Tac. We decided to rig one boat at a time.

First we laid out the mast and boom. The mast sits close to the bow of the boat. It came in two parts which and had to be slotted together then slid through a sleeve in the sail. With a bit of a struggle and a twang of complaint from my rib, Sam and I placed each mast, complete with sail, upright in a deep grove in the bottom of each boat. This is known as stepping the mast. The mast was then held upright and firmly in place by a gate locking mechanism.

The boom was then attached to the mast at right angles. The boom attachment which fitted around the mast is called a **goose neck**. The **downhaul**, which was attached to the bottom of the sail was fed though a hole in the goose neck and used to haul down the sail. This was to make it tight and as well as to secure the gooseneck. The downhaul was finally tied off on a K cleat on the mast. The halyard, which ran down the mast inside the sail sleeve, was pulled down tight to haul up the sail. The halyard was then wrapped round and secured by a K cleat on the outer side of the mast.

At the stern, the clew of the sail was secured to the **boom end** with two clips. One clip was for attaching the sail to the boom and the other also connected to the sail was then linked to the outhaul , a rope used to tighten the sail along the boom. The **outhaul** was then secured by a clam cleat (with teeth rather like a clam shell) on the boom.

The mainsheet was clipped onto a triangle of rope called the **horse** at the stern. When the horse is pulled tight and the loose end held in another clam cleat the boom is pulled down tightening the mainsheet which is fed up to the boom end, which then tightens the **leech** of the sail (the longest edge which when not tight is free to flutter) to increase the speed (increasing the "horse-power"). It was then fed along the boom and down to a pulley in the center of the boat and tied in a figure of eight knot so it did not slip out. From there the mainsheet is drawn in or out to control the movement of the sail.

Moving back towards the mast, along the boom was a clip attachment for one end of the **kicking strap**, a device with a cleat to hold the rope, and a pulley for it to run through as the kicking strap is loosened or tightened. This, the sailor adjusts while sailing to pull the boom down tightly or let it out depending on the winds and sailing direction. In high winds it is tightened to stop the boom from swinging wildly, it flattens the sail when pulled taut. In poor winds by easing or loosening the kicker it allows the boom to swing wide and for the sail to bag and capture more wind. The other end of the kicking strap is clipped fast onto the lower part of the mast.

Finally, at the furthest point on the stern, we had to fit the rudder attached by clips to the back of the dinghy. The rudder has an attachment called a *stock* to which is attached a tiller that the sailor holds to move the rudder and navigate the boat.

Along the way we had lots of discussion, some rather heated as the instructions were not always as straight forward as they first appeared. A prior knowledge of dinghy parts and rigging had been assumed in the instruction booklet. Undaunted, with Blue Tac fully rigged and her sail flapping skittishly around in the wind we followed the same procedure, a little wiser, and rigged Vitamin C.

We were eager to get the boats on the water and see how watertight they were. When I was in my twenties I had paddled, raced and taught the skills of canoeing using kayaks and Canadian canoes. Learning capsize drill and rescue techniques had been essential. That background and my being a strong confident swimmer helped a lot to allay our worries today. It was obvious even before our first sail that the Toppers were very tippy and with vague memories of my past Topper experience I was sure I would be spending time in the water.

With both boats rigged the wind was starting to pick up, the sails were fluttering and furling in anticipation, so we had to get moving. Sam pushed Blue Tack into the water and clambered aboard her with a jump and a roll. After a bit of twisting and turning as he fought to pull in the mainsheet and with the rudder tiller in hand he started to sail. He took her a little away from the shore and turned her around and back towards the shore, round and round making it look so easy.

He waited for me as I launched Vitamin C. As I grabbed for the mainsheet I was horrified to see that it had wrapped around the rudder. She swung round sharply, spinning out of my hand and capsized before I had even boarded her. Luckily I had kept hold of the mainsheet. Whilst she lay peacefully on her side in the water I clambered onto her upturned gunnels pushing down with all my weight to right her. She fought and fought me refusing to move.

The more I pushed, the more my rib screamed at me. As I battled on I realized she was resisting because she was swirling with water as the waves gushed over the bows. With one extra push her sail slowly lifted and with sucking and gurgling sounds she righted. By now the boat was full of water. But, ironically the extra weight stabilized her.

I hurled myself into the boat, clambering in, whilst holding tightly onto the tiller and the mainsheet. I winced as pain from my damaged rib raced through my body. I gritted my teeth as I pulled on the mainsheet and sheeted in and set the rudder. With one last burst of effort I pushed down the dagger board (similar to a centerboard for stabilizing the boat but is known as a dagger board as it travels up and down not back and forth), essential for keeping the boat stable. Then I was off! It felt fantastic as I flew across the water, even though I did not have a clue what I was doing.

Horrified, I realized I was rapidly approaching three expensive motor boats which were moored ahead of me. Vitamin C was feeling more and more like a wild stallion let out of its stable, hurtling me towards them. I prayed I would be able to weave a passage through them for I was certain that impact at this speed would create a LOT of expensive damage. Tears came to my eyes and clouded my vision as intense pain radiated from my rib. I pulled harder on the mainsheet. I had to lean backwards right over the edge of the boat to try and keep her hull in the water and keep control of her. I must keep her upright and get past the moored motor boats. Terrified, I gritted my teeth and hung on forcing myself to lean out further and further. Only my legs were in the boat now with my feet held fast by the toe straps. My whole body was leaning backwards out of the boat as I held her on a straight course. Then the exhilaration hit me. It felt fantastic!

Suddenly the wind dropped. I hauled myself back into the boat, exhausted. As I looked around me I was elated to see that I was already well beyond the motor boats. I could not believe I had slipped through the narrow passage between them.

I could see Sam in the distance and whilst I kept my eyes glued to him I could not help grinning with relief. Already he looked confident in Blue Tac. I followed his trail, trying to do what he was doing. We had invested in as many sailing books we could find, mostly from second hand stores. Although none of them focused on small boats, I had been avidly studying anyway.

However, reading and theory is one thing; actually putting theory into practice, particularly first time around, is another. For example I had a boat full of water but I could not remember how to use the boats manual bailer so the water stayed swooshing around in the boat. I decided that the best position to sit in the boat with a long swinging boom, as a novice, was in the center. With such a low boom at least I was not going to get tangled up in the sail! I felt rather like a baby, sitting in a bathtub of swirling, cold water rather than an intrepid sailor. I felt alone but not lonely. My recent sailing experiences up to this point had taken place with Sam near at hand, ready and eager to help and support me. Now it was time to move away from that dependency and sail solo. It felt empowering and terrifying yet vital for me and our developing team work.

Needless to say, with all that water swooshing about, my first deep water capsize was clearly imminent. As the wind picked up and the boat suddenly *heeled* (tilted with the windward side I was sitting on coming right out of the water), the boom end hit the water, the sail was next. I felt myself sliding forward, unable to stop myself. My first thought was to try to hit the water cleanly. I did not want to land on the sail or to get hit by the boom. As I felt myself slide under the sail, bits of boat came at me from all directions. I made direct contact with a number of them as evidenced by my later bruises. Trying to stay calm, pushing myself out from under the sail, I tried to recall the capsize drill I had ardently studied on the Topper website. I instinctively knew I must keep hold of the mainsheet. I then remembered that in order to right the boat I needed to keep hold of the mainsheet and swim around the hull, which was lying at 90 degrees to the water. I then had to reach up to the dagger board and haul myself up onto it. At this point I realized I had a problem, my rib. I gathered all my strength and on the third attempt hauled myself up. As I leaned across I felt an explosion of pain as my rib jammed up against the dagger board. I wanted to give up, slide off and howl with the pain but I breathed deeply and steadily to keep myself focused. With my legs dangling midair I had to find the inner strength to push and bounce. I lifted myself up onto my elbows and then hands to take the strain from the rib and using my full weight and determination pushed and bounced on the dagger board to lever it down towards the water and bring the sails out.

The pain in my rib tore through me but I kept on pushing down, using my hands and upper body weight as much as possible. I breathed a sigh of relief as the sails slowly released the water. As if in slow motion, the dinghy righted with much less water in it. Exhausted, I pushed myself up and over the gunnels, protecting my ribs as much as possible. As I clambered in and set sail the exhaustion slipped away and I felt light and empowered.

It had been tough and unpleasant but with the pain subsiding I felt enormously proud of my achievement. I could get myself out of trouble; I could right a capsized Topper without assistance. I felt elated and much more confident. I realized at that moment that the first capsize must be a make or break point for many would be sailors.

Thankfully I had made it and felt a strong desire to continue the sailing adventure, knowing that every day I sailed I would learn more and more. I had stepped up a notch in self esteem, driven by my desire to sail I have overcome the mental, emotional and physical challenge of my injury and had proved to myself that I could sail solo.

Deck Failure!

Friday July 20th

The Toppers fitted neatly onto the trailer, which Sam had now fitted with new wheels and bearings, so that we could take them back and forth, but the Hobie Wave was much too big and bulky to transport that way. Sam negotiated with Yannos at Columbia Water Sports, on Pissouri Beach, for enough beach space for the Hobie Wave to sit on alongside his boats. Columbia Water Sports, serves the Columbia Beach Hotel and Columbia Resort in Pissouri Bay.

First the Hobie Wave catamaran, "Kitty Moran" had to be assembled on her new beach space. When she was purchased and transported from Proteras, her mast was laid flat on her deck. Now, the first job was to bring the mast up and secure it with the shrouds. With pulling ropes attached and the mast roped up we hauled and hauled but the mast would NOT move. We gathered more helpers from the holiday makers on the beach, who had been watching our efforts with interest, but still no joy.

Sam examined the mast foot, which has a ball joint allowing the mast to pivot up to be righted and twist from side to side when sailing. He decided that it must have salted up and that corrosion glued one part of the hinge joint to the other.

Sam removed the mast foot, took it home and put it in a very, very hot oven. When he brought it out red and roasting hot he hit it with a sledge hammer. The salt caked corroded metal released. A desperate measure, but it worked!

By that afternoon we had the mast up and Kitty Maran was ready for rigging. Sam took me through the sailing procedure. The Hobie Wave does not have a jib and, thank heavens; there was no rudder extension either so from the beginning I knew this would be a much easier boat for me to learn on.

Once she was rigged we launched her for her first sail. I could tell immediately that she was much more stable than the Club 15, because being shorter yet about the same width across the beam she was more stable. In addition the hulls were much heavier so they did not lift out of the water quite so readily. This would make it easier to move across the decking.

Sam was thrilled to have a Wave to play with but he was aware that "Kitty Moran" had been standing around getting sun damaged for who knows how long. This was a boat trial and as Sam tacked and gybed he explained what he was doing and why. Being heavier and more stable, the Wave operated more slowly. This gave me more thinking time to assimilate each new action and co ordinate my movements. I drank in every word. The buckets of water still hurled over the bow but in the hot summer sun they had become welcome showers sending tingles of appreciation from head to toe. The wetter, the better!

We were in deep water, preparing to gybe when suddenly Sam's leg "disappeared" through the decking of the trampoline. Startled, we laughed! We assumed it was an isolated decking weakness due to aging in the sun.

Not so. We were scooting along as I scrambled across the deck ready for our next tack. Silently the decking gave way beneath me. I only just managed to grab the cross beam as I fell.

"Hang on", shouted Sam. "I am going to **hove to wind**" (the position in the wind were the boat has no sail power). Terrified I could feel my hands slipping. There was no grip on the wet shiny cross beam. The water was dragging at me. It was swirling around my waist pulling and grabbing at me. Sam yelled, "We must increase speed in order to turn and hove to. You must hang on!" I gripped onto the cross beam with all my remaining strength, while the sea eager to claim its prize pulled and tore at me.

We slowed as we **hove to.** As the catamaran stilled the sail began to flap playfully. Sheer relief welled up like a bubble and burst. I laughed helplessly with tears pouring down my face. Bemused, Sam hauled me out of the sea. I looked about and could see the holey mess. There was only a fragment of deck left, instead we had a chasm between two bows.

Today marked a breakthrough. Sam was astonished I faced the danger, hung on and rather than panicking saw the humour in the situation. He told me later that he would expect anyone else to give

27

up sailing. Instead I found surviving the immense power of the sea humbling and I was eager to continue.

Topper Challenges

With no Wave to sail we are back in the Toppers. Toppers are part of the dinghy class of boats, small, with one hull. Rigging and launching had become easier now.

The most challenging part for me was fitting the two sections of the mast the correct way round. Two spigots from one part slip into holes on the second part so I had to twist the mast around until it clicked. As the mast is slid through the sleeve of the sail it is vital to check which side of the top of the mast the sail hook hangs. When the upper section of the mast with the sail hook was the wrong way round I had to remove the sail and start all over again. It was both time consuming and frustrating. Both sections of the mast are long enough to be cumbersome and awkward to manoeuvre. My rib which seemed to have quieted a little complained loudly at the lifting and twisting action. Each failed attempt is painful, tiring and annoying.

Despite this my enthusiasm for sailing the Topper increased daily so I searched for an easily memorable solution. Eventually I discovered that the mast hook on top section must line up with the kicker strap hook on the bottom section. Using this same approach I began to tackle my list of ongoing rigging errors.

Sailing the Topper makes me think more independently about my sailing technique. Sam is literally there to guide me from afar, as the dinghies cannot be sailed too closely together until I have gained more experience. It was a perfect time to put myself under pressure to improve because the sailing conditions are perfect for learning and we have invested in rescue services from Yannos, just in case.

I began my practice in earnest. Sam set the objective for the day's sail and the achievement is up to me. I was however having two recurring difficulties. The first was failure to navigate effectively whilst bringing up the rudder and the dagger board as I come in to shore. The process seemed to require me to have three hands when I only have two and induced panic. The Toppers are old and the dagger board sat loose in its fitting and slipped back down when raised. It did not hold a middle position which meant that it usually has to be down or almost out.

Our beaching area is quite rocky. Depending on the approach, if I was too slow at pulling up the rudders or dagger board then they would get caught on the rocks and be damaged. Not only would these parts be costly but my Topper would be out of action for weeks, replacement parts would have to come from the UK.

Being aware of this challenge, Sam suggested fitting a device ingenious in its simplicity to both Toppers to help with the centerboard. It was an eraser cut into a wedge and attached to a rope. The wedge could be used to hold the centerboard in the different positions as needed and hold it there. When he fitted it, it worked perfectly. I could slot the wedge in and know the centerboard would stay in place releasing my need to use both hand and all the anxiety that went with it. The first time I used the wedge I sailed in for the first time with the feeling of being in control of my boat rather than the boat being in control of me.

The other difficulty I have was maintaining the accuracy of my *point of sail*. Sailing between two points requires a zigzag path as there is a "no-go zone" when directly facing the wind. It's usually about 90° (but in some conditions in Pissouri Bay can be as much as 120°) where the boat cannot sail because the wind is flowing past the sail. Sail boats can sail in any direction except directly into the wind. Sailing out with the whole bay in front of me offering a wide variety of options was easy, but sailing back to shore with a narrow window of beaching opportunity meant that, like all sailors, I had to zigzag from side to side. This maneuver is called **beating to windward** and involves repeatedly tacking through the "no-go zone" with clear reference points required for the next point you are heading relative to your final destination.

I simplified this to needing to know where my zig was going to end before I began my zag. The next challenge was to measure the combination of zigzags to get where I want to go. I had to predetermine exactly where I was going and maintain a plan on how to get there. Success eluded me. I loved sailing in Pissouri Bay but dreaded the humiliation of missing the final beaching point. I ended up in the rocks, in the swimming area or so far up the beach I had to drag the boat back through the water. Sam would be on the beach frantically waving and pointing in order to assist me. I was bemused as to why I was missing my target over and over again. I wanted to weep in frustration. I even missed the joy of success and the praise Sam showered on me when I did make it, because my success seemed to be random.

Black Rock Day

Tuesday July 24th

It was a breezy afternoon. Once we were out on the water the wind picked up and the sea conditions rapidly changed. I could feel through the rudder there was much more drag in the waves than I had previously experienced. My confidence began to dissolve. Every time I set my point of sail I was significantly off target. My anxiety welled up. I tried sheeting in to "close haul" which gives a much tighter control of direction but when tacking, the Topper heeled too much and I was in danger of capsize. I felt I had no control as she swung round. In order to avoid being hit by the boom I landed in the bottom of the boat over and over again. Each time I gathered myself together to sit precariously on the upper edge of the boat, which was at 70 degrees to the water, trying to balance it. I hauled at the mainsheet desperately trying to keep the mast out of the water. This would result in instant capsize. Whilst fighting with the waves, I was drifting north east across the bay. The pull of the sea was much stronger than the wind. I was not able to counter it. I tried time and time again to tack out to sea to get some wind but I could not get sufficient boat speed for the manoeuver. Already exhausted I began to tremble as I realized I could not turn the boat and head back towards the beach. Panic welled up inside me. With my jaw clenched I gripped the mainsheet tighter and held firmly onto the tiller. I was getting closer and closer to Black Rock Point, an array of sharp dragons teeth rocks. This was the last point before I reached the ominous rocky cliffs, the headland beyond which there was no landing point.

The more terrified I became the more I doubted my skills. Rather than **close haul,** I slowly let the sail out to about 90 degree, a **broad reach**, believing that this was scooping up as much wind as possible. I should have been doing the opposite instead, hauling the sail in as tight as possible to close haul to maximize the wind speed, in the battle with the fast moving, angry sea. I was not allowing the wind to help me. The sea continued to build and became a more agitated. I was being was dragged towards the jagged rocks at Black Rock Point.

I could see only cliffs and rocky outcrops ahead of me. I was desperately tired and looked around frantically for Sam. I had been so involved with my personal nightmare that I had lost track of him and had not given him any sign that I was having difficulties.

My confidence now in tatters I felt certain I could not manoeuver the boat around the rocks. I was now too close. Having capsized twice earlier that day I was tired and cold. A capsize close to rocks would be highly dangerous. I could easily be injured and the boat wrecked.

Feeling that I had no other option I clambered overboard holding onto the boat tightly whilst clutching the mainsheet. I aimed to swim and pull the boat ashore using what little wind there was behind me, to assist. Unfortunately the boat capsized within seconds once I had *bailed out,* (by sliding out of the boat and into the water). I tried to swim and drag the capsized boat and pull it towards the distant shore. Already exhausted I swam and swam. Pulling the boat was like dragging a weighty, stubborn anchor. It was too much for me. I was having difficulties staying afloat. I clung helplessly onto the boat and prayed.

I felt my prayers had been answered when close to the rocks I spotted two people. I waved frantically at them. Screaming and yelling, I shouted for help and waved my arms to show my distress. But they simply waved back. My pleas for help were lost in the wind.

In the distance I saw a flurry of sand and stones. A figure was running as straight as an arrow along the beach, hurdling over sunbathing bodies and heading in my direction. It was Sam! He HAD seen my distress.

The next moment he was clambering over the rocks. He yelled at me to hang on.

Within minutes a battered jeep came tearing along the beach. It screeched to a halt. Two young men dashed onto the rocks to join Sam. They conferred. The sea was too rough and dangerous. I was moving closer and closer to the dragons teeth, Black Rocks. As a very experienced swimmer, I knew I was in grave danger. The sea was rough enough to throw me against the rocks with great force.

The undertow of the rocks could suck me under and I was too weak to fight against it. I had to cling onto the boat.

The fittest of the young men dived in and began to swim towards me. Within minutes he had righted the boat. He was onboard and I was still clinging on helplessly with nowhere to go. He waved at someone behind me. A jet ski zoomed up, the rider, leaned over and plucked me out of the water. As the boat sailed away I could hear her bumping on the rocks. She was beached on a tiny piece of shoreline beyond Black Rock Point.

The Jet Ski rider took me to the beach where Sam was anxiously waiting. I sank down on my knees in the sand. He put his arms around me and I wept on his shoulder. Then Sam told me his experience.

Having seen the difficulties I was in, Sam had rushed to get a jet ski to rescue me. Yannos was not there. Instead Sam dashed full speed to rescue me himself. Sam's urgency alerted the young men with the battered jeep to join the rescue. Spurred on by all the activity, the Jet Ski rider came to my aid to complete the rescue.

What a day!

What an experience!

Thank you Sam for your heroism today! Thanks also to the rescue team who spontaneously came together, united by the urgency of the situation.

Catamaran Recovery

Saturday July 28th

The new cat deck arrived and we started fitting it with great enthusiasm. The decking was in three parts. First the two main deck sections had to be slid into the runners at the sides and then two slimmer sections of deck slid into the fore cross beams. To do this the hulls had to be separated and the cross beams had to be removed. Once the decking sections were attached the catamaran was reassembled. It was a tiring, fiddly, tedious job.

Next strong sturdy cord had to be laced attaching the two halves of the main deck as tightly as possible. The main deck then had to be laced to the aft section. Each threading had to be pulled super tight as it had to be firm enough to support our weight and be punched at by the sea.

Getting the cord though the holes was a problem, after the first few tries the cord began to fray. Sam dashed off to get some 'gaffer" tape from Yannos. We bound each cord end up with the plastic sticky "gaffer tape" making a sharp point at the ends to push through the holes with. We started making much faster progress.

We were each in charge of one of the two cords, which as with shoe laces, crossed over each other. We had to stop every now and again tugging really hard to make the cords as taut as possible. With Sam being much stronger than I, I had to make a lot more stops and tugs. It was exhausting work. My hands were already very sore from the pulling and tugging. Sam's fingers are much thicker than mine so threading the cord through the loops was an enormous challenge of patience for him. After a great deal of frustration on both sides we worked out a compromise. With my nimble fingers I threaded both cords and I then held onto them whilst Sam used his strength to tug and tightened. We continued with this team work until we got to the aft section. At the aft cross bar Sam went to the left and I went to the right. Still keeping the tension in the cords we had to continue threading over to one side and then back, crossing over the others handiwork. It was hot and fiddly but the end result was a strong and sturdy deck.

Eager to try out Kitty Moran, we set sail. The winds were strong and the waves were building. Within the bay the conditions are often turbulent, due to wind tunnels which funnel down through the surrounding hills and cliffs. There are also no-go points where these wind tunnels merge and cancel each other out. Once recognized these conditions could be avoided or exploited when a rest from the wind was needed. However, on days like today in addition the direction of the waves continuously changed which created mini wind vortexes at sea level. The wind could spin 180° or more in a second creating constant shifts and changes.

It soon became obvious that the design of the deck was faulty. The center gap which we had just spent almost two hours lacing was too wide. As soon as we launched the water shot up through the center section like a fountain and repeatedly soaked us. Worst of all, the pressure of the up-surging fountain of water continuously swept the mainsheet off the deck and through the gap leaving it trailing in the water behind us. During emergencies such as the danger of capsize, the mainsail has to be released to reduce the heeling motion and boat speed. The mainsheet has to have a free run to enable this. Eventually the mainsheet had to be gathered up and sat upon.

Beyond the bay, out at sea, the conditions were radically different. The waves were higher with the wind stronger and more consistent. I realized with great anxiety that we were heading out much deeper than before.

My building confidence in my sailing abilities had been badly shaken by my Black Rock Point experience. I was worried as we sailed for the first time beyond the bay and into higher waves. I could feel anxiety build as my stomach tightened as we sailed into the great unknown. I was terrified that no one would be able to see us if we got into difficulties. As I looked back I could see the impressive buildings of the Columbia Beach Hotel and Resort getting smaller and smaller.

I had every confidence in Sam. It was *my* ability I was concerned about. My head was buzzing with worries and fear. What if we capsized? We had not practiced the capsize drill. I had no idea how to right the catamaran. I doubted if I could. How would I react in such an emergency? What if Sam fell overboard or got injured? Could I sail the boat well enough to rescue him?

Unlike a car you cannot slam the brake on in an emergency. All boats continue to move away from the "man over board" referred to as **MOB**, even when you slow down in the hove too position. There is a special procedure taught by the RYA, on how you sail past the MOB and then in a controlled way navigate a figure of eight manoeuvre to return and collect them. I had read about it, but I had no idea how to put it into practice.

I had had little helming practice on this catamaran. The Hobie Wave was very different from the Hobie 15. By this time I was literally wringing my hands with worry. My teeth were beginning to chatter although it was not cold. Sam noticed and asked if I had a problem. When I explained he laughed.

"This is how you learn" he said. "Forget the books you have to get out there and sail. I know you can do it".

Sam encouraged me to helm and talked me through tacking and gybing the Hobie Wave. We linked the maneuvers together to make a figure of eight in preparation for MOB practice. I began to feel a little better. The Hobie Wave does not have a jib only a mainsail, therefore she moves much slower than the Hobie 15. She is much more solid to handle as she has heavier hulls and sits lower in the water. The two catamarans were as alike as a cart horse and a young Arab stallion.

Although I was grateful for the figure of eight and MOB practice, I was not too sure about being in the deeper water. What a relief it was to see the Columbia Hotel coming into sight once more as we sailed back.

I felt exhausted from the anxiety and relieved when the day's sail was over. Was I losing my confidence altogether?

Once we had packed our sailing gear away I shared my concerns with Sam. He confided in me that he was always anxious when he sailed, particularly when having to consider the safety of another person, me. It is a necessary part of sailing. He agreed to add "man overboard" practice to our agenda as soon as possible. I felt buoyed by the positive result from our frank discussion.

To Cape Aspro

Tuesday July 31st

What a wonderful evening!

As a child growing up in England I used to love the BBC Sunday World Service weather report. Conditions at Cape Aspro and Cape Greko were always mentioned. Although I had no idea where these places were, the names sounded foreign and exciting. It is extraordinary that I now live just down the road from Cape Aspro. How wonderful to be here in Cyprus sailing in these waters!

The sea was gentle but with enough wind to sail. We took the Hobie Wave, Kitty Moran, out beyond the Pissouri Bay towards Cape Aspro. It was the deepest we had sailed. It felt as if we were in the open sea even though we could see the steep forbidding cliffs of Cape Aspro.

It was early evening. I felt much more confident after my talk with Sam a few days ago and I did not feel as nervous. I helmed for half an hour. I felt for the first time that I was in control, focused and really enjoying myself even though I was mesmerized by the changing colours of the sea and sky as they shifted in harmony from pale pink to rose and then magenta.

Each time we sailed we were pushing our boundaries of the accumulating experiences of time, distance and territory. We sailed for longer, sailed much further and explored new areas. Each sail therefore seemed less daunting. As the new became the familiar, I hoped that eventually the familiar would not become mundane. Sailing is adding a whole new dimension to my life, challenging me in ways I would not have thought possible.

It may sound arrogant but over the last few years I worked hard and overcame the challenges of my car accidents. I built a thriving business in Cyprus, expanding the new field of complimentary therapies with my Feldenkrais Practice. I suffered the loss of that impetus because of my extensive recovery time from the accident in 1998, over 8 years. Knowing that precious time could not be recovered, instead I focused on completing my Master in Education (Inclusive Education/Special Needs) to expand the range of those I could help. I have confidence in the knowledge that I have proved to myself that I am brave, resilient and tenacious.

Learning to sail was putting me right back on the starting block. I had to rebuild my confidence, bravery and resilience to fit totally different parameters.

Developing Confidence

Wednesday August 1st

Back to West Winds Water Sports in Limassol for another destination sail in the Hobie 15, Sam's "Kitten Cat".

I feel that great progress is being made as I helmed during most of the sail today. I still became confused but was less concerned about the confusion. I am learning to analyze less. As I trust more in my growing body of knowledge and experience, my responses are becoming more innate.

I love the smooth, catlike body movements and transition that Sam has demonstrated again and again. I felt comfortable, almost at ease, as I turned to face the aft of the boat, moved the rudder bar and shifted my position around the moving sail to tack and gybe.

My ticking mind and heart-crushing anxiety were no longer making me behave like a fool and feel incompetent. Although I loved to sit beside Sam as he helmed, I loved the feeling of independence when I took the helm. There were times when I felt like the master of the ship, guiding her, turning her and setting sail to the next point.

Excruciating Success

Friday August 3rd

Today, as helm, I launched the Wave, Kitty Moran in Pissouri for the first time. As we pulled her close to the water's edge I felt really anxious but below the anxiety were effervescing bubbles of excitement ready to explode.

Together we lifted her hulls and turned her into the wind ready to rig her. In this position there is minimal pull or drag on the sail so rigging is much easier and there is less chance of the boat being blown over. Once rigged, as we pulled her into water, we needed the water deep enough for the rudders to come down safely. Sam turned her to point a little closer to the wind and then climbed aboard.

I held onto her hull then scrambled over the stern with the now familiar ouch from my rib. As helmsman I had to immediately take control of the rudder bar and mainsheet and turn her close to the wind, which had just picked up. From this point I could get the catamaran in motion to complete the launch.

As we began to sail I had to avoid Yannos's Rescue Boat, ski boat, jet skis and large inflatable water toys moored in the area. Thankfully today there were no swimmers, as they often stray into the area, too. Holding my breath, with my hand on the rudder and my heart in my mouth we were off. I let her fly.

With her close-hauled, as close to the wind as possible which was just before the edge of the "no-go zone", we shot out.

I sheeted in the sail tightly as Sam had taught me. The mainsheet can be held fast and cleated but the rudders have to be held firmly. The Wave did not have a rudder extension at this time so I had to position myself so that I could reach the rudder bar. I tried to make my rib as comfortable as possible but there was always a background ache when I was helming.

As we got closer to the wind, the windward hull began to lift. I panicked and was about to release the sail a little but Sam shouted, "Sheet in! Sheet in!" The hull lifted even more as we sped out to sea. It was incredibly exciting. We went faster and faster as I desperately clung to the rudder bar battling with the force of the torrents of water which were pummeling the rudders trying to pull us off course. Exhausted, I brought her out of the wind, slowed her to gybe and brought her fully about. The next moment the hull was up as we sailed into the wind once more. This was a totally exhilarating experience demanding an enormous amount of strength and concentration. As I held on fast to the rudder bar and mainsheet my rib felt as if it was burning. It felt like a burning hot anvil, which, fueled by the body tension, was getting hotter and hotter and sending searing pains like white hot sparks everywhere. It demanded that I limited the use of my core strength. Impossible under these conditions! Unable to hold the boat on course any longer, I had to hand over to Sam.

I was both elated and bitterly disappointed. The wind had been perfect, the catamaran sailing perfectly in ideal conditions. I loved the speed and intensity. The rush of adrenaline gave the feeling of being one with everything, the sea, the catamaran, the wind and Sam. Everything merged.

Everything except that pesky erupting rib!

Solo at Last!

Saturday August 4th

I attempted my first solo sail in the Wave today. Sam and I launched the Wave together and I was looking forward to helming once more, then unexpectedly, he turned, smiled and said, "Drop me off at the beach. You are ready to solo sail. Take as long as you want".

It was perfect practice weather, gusting Beaufort Scale Force 2, the sea was creating small wavelets and I could feel the wind softly tickling my skin as it moved brushed across my arm. Nothing too challenging.

With great excitement, clutching onto the rudder bar and mainsheet I sailed her out. Checking over my shoulder I could see the Columbia Hotel getting smaller and smaller. I was astonished that I was not afraid. Knowing there was no hurry and the gentle wind was on my side I brought her bow across the "no-go zone" and tacked, changing the direction I was sailing in. I tacked again and again. Buzzing with excitement I turned the stern of the catamaran through the "no-go zone" and gybed.

I was feeling more and more confident by the minute, when, during my next maneuver the rudder attachment slipped and lifted the port rudder up. I jiggled it as I had been shown. It would not re-engage. I tried again and again but the rudder stayed jammed. Now the catamaran was floundering. She did not know which direction to go. I tried to keep her into wind, the most stable position, but I needed both hands to try and manoeuver the rudder attachment. I was aware the boat was spinning this way and that. Determined to find a solution, I clambered over the rudder bar and wriggled up the hull to the furthest point I could reach. I leaned right over the back of the boat to try and see why the attachment was locking out. Hanging on with my knees, I used both hands to tease the rudder attachment back into position so that the rudder could drop. I tried over and over again until, exhausted, I had to clamber back onto the deck.

I realized I had to try and sail her back with one rudder fully in the water and the other just skimming the surface. This would not be too much of a problem if I was sailing "close haul" into the wind. Then the windward hull would be the port hull and would be out of the water. The rudder would be out of the water anyway. However the wind was behind me and so I was on a run. Both rudders needed to be in the water as this is the least stable direction.

With my stomach in a knot my mind whirred as I tried to remember all I had learnt to this point. I was sure that a more experienced sailor would easily find a solution. With my confidence evaporating at a great rate of knots I realized that the wind was dropping. I needed to bring Kitty Moran back in quickly using the route through the boating lane of Yannos's Water Sports area. But, try as I might, I could not get her to sail in the correct direction.

I could see Sam on the beach waving his hands to direct me where I was supposed to land. He was pacing back and forth. He must have seen me stall her and had wrongly assumed that I had lost my confidence. Close to tears I had no choice other than to bring the boat in through the forbidden swimming area. With a face like thunder Sam waded out to me, and without a word climbed aboard. He took the helm and snapped at me to leave the boat and go to the beach. Devastated, I slid off the catamaran. I wanted the sea to swallow me up. Feeling totally abandoned and wretched I slowly waded to the shore. I understood the urgency of moving the boat out of the swimming area and into the boat lane but why did I have to leave the boat? I was being treated like a naughty child and, frankly, felt like one.

As Sam sailed away I watched downheartedly as he deftly jiggled the rudder back into place. As he came about I could see him stall the boat and "hove to". It looked as if the rudder was up again. As he was close to shore I could see him struggling, leaning over the bow just as I had. I felt sure he was having the same problems. He then smoothly came about and brought the boat in through the boat lane. As I walked up to him I could see that he was furious.

He was convinced that he had pushed me too hard. He thought I just did not have what it takes to sail solo. To sail together we both needed to be confident that the other could take over in an emergency.

As he glared at me I pointed out to him that I had done everything possible to release the rudder attachment. I had not given up at the first obstacle as he thought. Even though I was still in the early stages of learning to sail solo I had had the confidence to bring an ailing boat back into shore although sadly by the wrong route. I could feel the heat of my pent up frustration. I tilted my chin and raised my voice as I looked him in the eye and said, "I am proud of myself today. I did not give up. I did the best I could do with the experience and knowledge I have gained to date". At that point more than any to date I felt I had the tenacity, determination and resilience to sail.

As I understand it, sailing is a unique combination of the precociousness of the wind, shifting, variable sea conditions, a seaworthy boat, an experienced helm with a confident crew and lots of sailing experience. Add to these masses of patience as these elements blend together teasing, taunting and trying to tame each other. As Sam has pointed out to me numerous times it is important to go out and do it. Making mistakes is a vital part of the learning process. The important thing is to be able to go back and try again. I most certainly will.

After all it WAS my first attempt at sailing solo.

GREAT Sailing Day

Sunday August 5th

I am painfully aware that yesterday would definitely have been my last sailing day with Sam had I not stood up for myself. What I experienced out on the water was, I believe a courageous attempt to get an ailing boat operational. Rather than considering my first solo sail as a failure, I saw a glimmer of personal success.

What Sam saw from the shore was a floundering boat being sailed by, what appeared to be, an incompetent solo sailor. He then watched horrified as I sailed a 13 foot catamaran into the swimmers' area of a 5 star hotel. I could not dispute what he saw. My only way forward was to replace that embarrassing image with one of me proving myself as a committed solo sailor and confident crew.

Happy to be given another chance, I felt more determined to rise to the challenge than ever before. Today the winds rose to the occasion and were powerful enough to make it a really exciting sail.

Sam demanded from the start that I helm. I tacked and gybed and gybed and tacked. Round in circles and back on myself I went, creating figures of eight over and over again. This is an essential manoeuver for man over board (MOB) rescue. If someone goes overboard you must continue to sail about ten boat lengths then you tack bringing the boat back and round to the MOB on a **broad reach** with the sails at about 45 degrees to the boat, 90 degrees to the wind with the MOB on the windward side of the boat otherwise the heavy boat could crash in to the MOB.

I sailed way out to sea. I tackled high waves and strong winds. I kept her on course, sheeted in, gritted my teeth against the pain and used all my strength. I sailed as close to the wind as I could, knowing that with one slight twitch in the wrong direction and it would be very difficult to regain control.

Sam had made it quite clear that if we were going to sail together he had to know he could rely on me to keep my head, no matter what the conditions. As I brought Kitty Moran into the boat lane to return Sam nodded and I could see the twitch of a smile as he said, "Well done, a great day for you".

There were times today when I felt that I was one with the boat. We were moving together like dancing partners, I was guiding and she was following, both elated. There were other times when I was truly terrified, almost overwhelmed by the enormity of the sea and the waves. I realized that at these times I had separated myself from the flow of sailing, I was no longer sensing the wind on my face or the cooling spray of sea water. I simply wanted to force the boat to do my will and survive. Exhausted, with an enormous smile on my face I knew it had been a GREAT day.

Trip to "Triton"

Wednesday August 8th

Sam bought a large wooden boat in April this year, "Triton". She is moored in Larnaca Marina. Our first visit was on May 9th which was my birthday surprise from Sam. We had been travelling to Larnaca most weeks since then for one or two overnight stays.

"Triton" was a mythological Greek God, the son of Poseidon and Amphitrite, god and goddess of the sea respectively. He is usually represented as a sea-hued merman with his shoulders barnacled with sea-shells. Over time the name Triton became associated with a class of mermaid-like creatures, the Tritons, which could be male or female, a race of sea gods and goddesses born from Triton.

Triton is a 56 foot traditional motor sailor with a wooden mast, lovely wooden interior and she sleeps four. I loved her on sight!

I was captivated by her beautifully rounded stern, topped with curvaceous carved, wooden railings with a gated center gap for the gangplank. Gingerly walking across the gangplank, I stepped over the curved seating area which followed the flowing lines of the hull. Straight ahead are the doors to the cabin which houses the cockpit. Stepping through the doors, the ship's wheel is the first thing you see. Its dark golden wood and classic lines tell something of Triton's 40 year old history. She is a Turkish, Bodrum-built boat.

The interior is well lit but smelt very musty, with front and side windows as well as galleon style side lights. To the right is a plush, soft cream sofa. The wood inlaid instrument panel sits beside the ships wheel. The walls and cabin roof are beautifully wood paneled in mahogany. This rich wooden, organic theme continues throughout the boat.

Straight ahead is an opening with steps leading down into the well equipped galley. The cooking area to the left is efficient yet discreet with the sink, refrigerator and hob hidden beneath perfectly fitting wooden inserts so that when not in use it is a clutter free worktop. To the right is a sofa which doubles as a single bunk. Beyond the galley to the left is a cabin with one bunk and straight ahead from the galley is the fore-cabin which the mast passes through. This cabin houses two single bunks. To the right of the galley, opposite the single cabin is the "heads", the seaman's name for toilet and shower.

I understand Sam's enthusiasm. He bought her as a refurbishment and renovation project. At that time, the wood throughout had a layer of black, grey mould and the cream coloured soft furnishings were grey tinged with mould and smelled horribly musty. When Sam stripped the ceiling panels we found that the undersides were thick with grey, black mildew which also coated the inside of the revealed cabin roof.

Over a sequence of earlier visits I had scrubbed and cleaned the roof interior and all the soft furnishing including the curtains which had seemed initially to be beyond hope, but with tender loving care they recovered. The sleeping cabin roof panels were replaced and luckily the bed heads and the sofas soon regained their soft, sweet smelling creaminess. Unfortunately the sleeping mats had to be completely remade. Tempting though it was to choose a fabric that was modern and bright we kept within the style of the boat with a silver grey washable, yet hardy, fabric.

Sam worked on the woodwork, repairing damaged areas using ingenious techniques which he had developed when working on car repairs. He looked at the grain, texture and surrounding areas and used beeswax, candle wax and boot polish, massaging and blending them in layer by layer to bring the wood back to its former glory. I helped where I could. As Sam worked his magic and repaired, cleaned and polished the wood until the interior shone, he then and added brass fixtures which had belonged to his family home. He hung a brass bell, ornate clothes hangers, clocks and ornaments such as a brass anchor and ship's wheel which had waited for lifetimes to find the right home.

Triton is now a home from home that I love to spend time on. I love the compact uncluttered space. Everything from the galley stove to the heads is neat, clean and functional. The wooden paneling throughout now glowed with a golden light.

As it was a hot humid night Sam took his bedding mat onto the cabin roof to sleep under the flickering stars, alone. I could hear him moving about as he settled directly above me
As I lay in my bunk, rocked by the moving water beneath, Triton creaked and sighed as she pulled at her moorings. I dreamed of voyages to come, perhaps to the Greek islands or even beyond.

Crystal Cool Waters

Thursday August 9th

Triton is temporarily moored in the visitor's quay. Today she was the only boat there and we had the bay to ourselves.

Before breakfast we had decided to put down the ladders and swim from the boat. The turquoise water glittered with early morning light and was wonderfully cool and refreshing. The water was so still and clear, almost glasslike, as if looking through a window. As I swam I saw shoals of tiny multi coloured fish darting about beneath me and beneath them the larger darker coloured solitary fish lurking. Suddenly a turtle popped its head up, looked at me startled and quickly swam away.

I love being at the marina. The chitter, chatter of the halyards against the metal masts is a continuous background chorus as, caught by the breeze, masts sway rhythmically

Walking along the quay is a leveling experience for me. There are multi-million euro motor cruisers moored next to historic sailing yachts, traditional motor boats, motor sailing boats like "Triton" and simple family day boats. Each has their place. Nothing stays the same. There is a constant flow of boats venturing on their next extraordinary journey, each one with gripping stories to tell.

Deeper and Deeper Still

Friday August 10th

Once again in Pissouri, we sailed even further in "Kitty Moran", beyond the headland and out into much deeper waters. The sea moves differently once outside the bay. There is a rolling motion, a constancy that is missing when we sail closer to shore. Today I truly felt we were sailing in the Mediterranean. The hues of the sea shift and change back and forth from deep blue to a soft gentle powder blue with patches of turquoise, as the waves with their powerful swell, tumble and roll.

As I helm I can feel the constant tug on the rudders. Like two squabbling children, the sea and the wind pull and tug at the catamaran. As intent as a resolute parent, I am determined that neither will get their way. With my confidence blossoming, my actions are clearer as I firmly encourage them to work together, certain that I will not yield but ready to move with the flow until they can meld and meet harmoniously.

This level of focus and concentration is tiring. After some time, exhausted but determined not to move into fear and anxiety, I hand the helm over to Sam. As I do so I feel a flash of understanding and also of deep respect for Sam's endeavours in teaching me so far. Sailing is exciting and challenging but it is not easy. It will never be easy. It is vital for me to be driven less by my chattering thoughts. I want to become more intuitive. I need to trust myself enough to feel the wind, listen to the sound of the rudders as they cut through the water and to the humming of the sails. I need to let them tell me what to do next, rather than fearfully inflicting my will on them.

Sam catches my eye, nods and smiles. He knows I have grasped something significant, something that will have an immense impact on my future as a sailor.

Rib Revival

Saturday August 11th

The winds are just right today at Force 3 South-Westerly the sea was making large wavelets and occasionally they crested and formed whitecaps as the wind built slightly.

These are perfect conditions to practise. We set off for the deeper water again. In fact we are sailing further from land than we have sailed to date. We switch helm and when it is my turn Sam sets a direction for me to follow with the intention that I hold the course.

My rib pain, although most of the time a little less intrusive, limits me on the helm during these more challenging conditions. There is such a powerful pull on the rudders that I have to use all my strength to hold the catamaran on a steady course. I am fine when we are on a port tack, with me sitting on the left side of the catamaran and the wind coming over my left shoulder. My right arm controls the rudder bar and my body is twisted bringing diagonal tension on my lower left rib which is not injured. However, on the starboard tack, sitting on the right side of the boat with the wind coming over my right shoulder, my left arm is on the rudder bar and my body twist is pulling on the lower right injured rib. This pressure is excruciatingly painful. Therefore I can sail in one direction but not in the other. I feel limited and frustrated.

Unfortunately, the osteopath I have been visiting regularly believes I keep re-injuring the same spot. He wants me to take time out of sailing. I am NOT prepared to do that at this time. I have the opportunity to sail NOW. Who knows what the next months will bring? Sam is already talking about moving to Larnaca to work more intensively on Triton. If I take time out of sailing now, that could bring that decision forward. I would lose both the opportunity to sail and a man I am beginning to care about deeply. It would be a heartbreaking.

Despite the pain and frustration, I am aware that adapting to the rib pain has helped me to develop greater movement awareness. I have learnt to move more smoothly, fine tuning my catlike movement across the decking.

Perhaps the pain is helping to improve my sailing by sharpening my awareness of what I do and how I do it. Teachers come in many guises.

At Last!

Sunday August 12th

Sam has been encouraging me to refine my ability to pick up wind direction through feeling the wind on my back, the back of my neck, the side of my face and even my hand. I have been practicing all the time as a daily exercise, even when not sailing. Stopping and pausing wherever I am. I turn my cheek or reach out and feel the wind with the palm or back of my hand. I am excited that already I am sensing the shifts and changes of even gentlest of winds. I am also looking at all the other clues around me, paying close attention to the movement of the branches in trees, smoke from the power station chimneys, flags and even dust picked up by the wind.

Many dinghy sailors have been taught to depend on "telltales". Telltales are small lengths of wool or ribbon which, when attached to specific points of the sail, stream out with the wind running across their backs. Red is on the port side of the sail and green is on the starboard side. The objective is to have them both streaming out in a similar way. Telltales show the actual movement of the wind across the sail's surface. As the wind hits different parts of the sail, as it flows across the sail, it has to make compromises. These compromises can often slow the boat down or even bring the boat to a stall. Stalling is invisible, as the sail will keep its airfoil shape but will not produce enough power to provide the forward momentum. This happens if sailing too far into the wedge of "no wind" and is called "sailing too close to the wind". The best aspect is to be as close to the wind as possible but with maximum power. This is a fine line to find and to maintain. Then, not only does the boat gather speed but there is more overall control of the boat for the sailor.

Unfortunately the telltales, cannot be relied on as they often get stuck against the sail through either a buildup of static or the fibers of the sail stitching grabbing the fibers of the tell tale. Picking up the wind direction innately is easier when the wind is strong and steady but in Pissouri Bay we often get swirly winds and gusts.

These daily exercises in reading the wind are helping me to fine-tune my wind awareness. It is a breakthrough that fills me with joy. Sam has been convinced that these finely-tuned senses are something that only some people are born with. I, however, am sure that they are accessible to us all, as they are senses that our ancestors relied on. Sadly, most of us have forgotten we have them, as they have diminished in importance in our daily lives. I believe that they can be re-learned. To reconnect with Nature on such a deep level is not only empowering, it is liberating. It is another step towards one of my great passions, developing the highest possible level of self reliance. I believe this is key to our human survival on planet Earth.

Special Delivery

Tuesday August 14th

I was becoming so immersed in sailing, particularly when sailing solo in the Topper that time simply disappeared. Timing our journeys had become more and more important, particularly as we are discovering at this time of the year that there are patterns of wind shifts which can be as much as 180°, gusts or the wind drops completely.

Experience has taught me that it is as challenging sailing in strong winds as it is being out there becalmed in the baking sun. Strong winds are exhausting. The static energy due to the muscle tension required to hold the mainsheet tight and constant is huge. Toppers do not have a mainsheet cleat so as I have held on tightly with the mainsheet wrapped around my hand it has sometimes been so excruciatingly painful I have prayed for the next phase; my hand going numb with the tension and restricted blood flow. Added to that the enormous amount of dynamically focused concentration involved, it is easy to tire.

It is becoming clear to me that a high level of fitness is essential not only to sail boats but to move them from place to place. For the uninitiated and without beach trailers, Toppers are awkward to carry and heavy. The two catamarans, which do have beach trailers, demand plenty of strength and flexibility to get them onto the beach trailers then focus and stamina to move them around. In order to build up my strength and particularly my stamina I have begun a program of exercises. I am sure the program will keep on developing along with my needs.

Sail boats are dependent on the wind. In order to find the right position in the wind for your boat to maximize the potential to get where you want to go, you have to find the "correct point of sail" which means literally just that. You want your sail and therefore the bow of your boat to point where you want to go and not waver. Loss of concentration creates less clarity in direction which means, already tired, you may have to add an extra tack at the end of your journey. In order to do so you may have to sail back out to sea. To maximize the wind you are sailing at an angle which takes you back on yourself in order to come in at the correct angle to shore. To do this in Pissouri Bay you have to sail out of the bay to catch the "true wind" rather than the wind induced by the bay's land formation. This can take fifteen minutes, often more to perform and can be really dispiriting.

When the wind drops the drive power for the boat is lost. Not only have you lost the power to move forward but you have also lost the power to navigate. A sailboat needs to be moving in order to turn. Without that drive you end up drifting helplessly. On a scorching hot day you can get dehydrated quickly as well as sunburnt. I have only been becalmed twice, luckily right at the end of the day's sailing. The first time I followed Sam's example of using the rudder like the fin of a fish moving it back and forth. When this is done gently enough a little forward motion can be gained but a lot of patience is needed. Ideally, we should have a set of oars but as Toppers are so small they do not have any space for storage. They are designed to be sailed on inshore water such as reservoirs and dams. Therefore, they would not be too far from the shore. However, sailing on coastal waters as we do, this is not the case.

When I went down to the village post office today I was delighted to find that the Royal Yacht Association (RYA) sailing books that we had ordered have arrived. Our waterproof Rotary diving watches have also arrived. I could hardly wait to try mine on and put it into use.

As I tore the paper off the packages Sam watched in amusement. Then, with my watch resplendent on my wrist I chose "Go Sailing – A practical handbook for young people" the RYA children's book to flick through first. I bought it with its companion, "Go Sailing Activity Book for Young Sailors". It looked perfect for my needs being simply written, colourful, with wonderfully clear diagrams. We also had copies of RYA's "Start Sailing" which tied in with their Level 1 and 2 Training Course. Each manoeuver is explained both for sailing dinghies and for catamarans, which allows for the necessary different techniques for the different types of boats. For future reading I had also purchased RYA's "Competent Crew" a more advanced book for offshore yachting.

We were immediately immersed in the books, reveling in the opportunity to check up on the procedures the RYA recommends and their training requirements and to tie them in with what we had already discovered by being out on the water on an almost daily basis.

Sailing Satisfaction

Saturday August 18th

Having studied our new sailing books for a few days it was fantastic to be out today. The books have taken some of the pressure off Sam. Now he can simply say, "Go. Check it out" when I have questions. The books have already helped me to answer some of my inner struggles.

My struggles relate to information I have not quite grasped and questions I have not been able to put into words. These focus around the challenge of getting my Topper to shore exactly where I want to. Even having followed all the guidance Sam has given me, I am frequently off target and have to go out and tack again. At other times I sail in perfectly.

But what have I done so differently? I know a boat can sail sideways but sometimes it feels as if the boat is ALWAYS slipping sideways across the water just as a novice skier side slips across the snow. The other frustration I have is tacking the Topper. Often I get stuck in the "no go area". I am unsure how I only manage to turn the boat a little but not far enough to be under sail once more. This leaves me with the boat floundering *in irons*, stuck in the "no-go zone", unable to move her to the left or right until a chance gust of wind gives the assistance to complete the turn.

With the books at hand I can now delve in and explore the how's, whys and wherefores at my own pace. This will enrich my sailing. Already Sam has taught me so much. I know I have gaps in learning. There have been times when something made absolute sense on one day, then, under different conditions it made no sense at all. As I was not sure what I have misunderstood it was difficult to backtrack and uncover the question. Going through the books methodically will, I am sure, help me to fill in the gaps. This means I can maximize on the opportunities of being on the water and develop my skills further with Sam.

My directional confusion could be related to my dyslexia, as in everyday life I have challenges with identifying my right and left.

Most dyslexics learn well through making greater uses of their five senses. The RYA "Go Sailing - Practical Handbook for Young Sailors" and the "Go Sailing - Activity Book for Young Sailors" are excellent for dyslexic sailors, since they are multi-sensory and encourage the use of creativity and imagination to find acronyms to help remember important points. I discovered I could easily remember that, port wine being red, makes it easy to recognize that the red coloured "tell tales" is the port one. To make link with the left side, I tell myself "there is no port left".

When you are out at sea the conditions can change so suddenly, that they can take you by surprise. It is at such times you realize the wildlife around you has a far greater understanding of what is happening and is already preparing for what is to come. Some years ago I watched my cats stop mid stride and go rigid for seconds then turn in unison to look at me in warning a few minutes before an earthquake shook my home. It was eerie. Recently, I noticed how the sparrows simply disappear from their usual habitat for days before a cold spell and reappear days later when the sun comes out again. How do they know? Where do they go?

All these creatures have maintained and continued to develop their highly evolved senses in order to survive. We, however, have grown dependent on the TV weatherman, our computers and apps to tell us what the weather will bring, when the storms are going to roll in and when snow is expected. We have allowed technology to dull our senses. We have been lulled into believing that our lives no longer depend on the vagaries of the planet's weather patterns. We have lost the desire to use and fine tune these essential skills.

I began my journey of reclaiming myself by learning to sense the wind. It was the beginning of reclaiming and recognizing other natural skills and developing another type of self confidence. It is sense that comes from deep within. I am beginning to understand that when we use our five senses to tune into the world around us we connect with a knowing, an understanding. Fears begin to drop away as we become more self reliant. It is as if the fears well up from insecurity driven by a resistance to use our innate skills leading to a disconnection from the elements, the animals, the plants, the sea, absolutely EVERYTHING.

Magical Mountains

Sunday August 19th

The bright sunny days meant we were getting hotter and hotter on the water. Sam and I were ready for a day off. Today we decided to visit the mountain reservoirs. As the Toppers are easily transported on the road trailer, we were eager to explore the reservoirs as potential sailing locations.

First stop was Aspro Kremous Dam, to the right of Pissouri and set in the hills opposite Timi Village. During heavy winter rains the reservoir overflows creating a dramatic waterfall which then cascades into the dry river bed below and out to sea.

As we turned off the main road, we began a steep climb up an extremely dusty, bumpy track. It was hard work even for Sam's Suzuki. At the top, we stopped and stared with amazement at the immense expanse of water that lay before us. Flat and still with just a whisper of wind, I felt as if we were in another world. Everywhere around us was brown, barren, rugged and rocky. The blue water twinkled and winked, adding to the impression that it was simply an illusion.

Although it was a perfect spot for sailing light dinghies, there was no shade whatsoever. It would be very hot on the water for although there would be wind, without sea current, there would be fewer waves. The heat would be searing from the unbroken reflection of the sun. The access road was poor and there were no launching points, just jagged rocks. The fishermen sitting amongst the rocks did not look too friendly either. They scowled at us and as they turned their backs we scurried back to the car and drove on.

The next stop was Archbishop Makarios's Village, Panagia. As we approached the cool, tree lined mountain village, it was already busy with coaches and busses carrying tourists visiting the monastery and churches. The mountain streams, which brought life to the village, could be faintly heard splashing, tinkling and dancing in the background. We stopped for a drink at a very lovely little road side café. Sitting on the sunny corner we had an enviable view of the mountains and the village square. The host was very friendly and brought us some home-made cakes with our tea. We were not hungry but assuming they were gratis, we ate one each, simply to be polite. When we got the bill we had been outrageously overcharged. What a shame!

Disappointed, we travelled on. We could see the next reservoir in the valley below us. We tried to ignore the jarring of the bumpy unmade road as it took us through a flickering canopy of green foliage. The plant-life was rich, verdant and glorious. The rattling of the Suzuki could hardly be heard above the crashing and rushing of water as the streams bounded down the mountain into the reservoir. Yet it felt peaceful. I yearned to clamber over the rocks and slip into the inviting cool of the water and float under the shade of the trees. It is a heavenly spot, but once again without any launching or easy access points. Undaunted, I imagined the Toppers silently slipping through the water, as we sailed from shady bank to shady bank on a blazing hot day such as this, cool and undisturbed.

We spotted a track leading up towards Cedar Valley, named after the cedar forest which covers the whole area. Sam began to manoeuvre the Suzuki up the steep rugged track. I held on tightly to the handle above the door. Sam's past experience as a farmer got us out of sticky situations time and time again as she slewed across the road. We slipped and slithered on the water-splashed track wending our way to Troodos.

We were in the middle of nowhere when Sam suddenly braked and pulled over. He turned to me. Deeply concerned, he had remembered he had evicted the spare wheel to create space for our sailing equipment on our last sailing day. We were in isolated and treacherous territory without a spare wheel. What should we do? Go back or carry on?

We could hear the mountain streams bubbling and gurgling their approval, as with fingers crossed, we continued even more cautiously.

As we drove up the steep hills to Cedar Valley we came across a small plateau. Before us was a beautifully laid out, public picnic area and camp site with a stream running through. The wooden cabins were new. It was impressively clean and orderly but deserted. The cool dampness of the mossy mountain rivers and flickering dappled lights of the sun through the trees and foliage made it an idyllic getaway from the roasting summer sun.

We travelled on for over an hour and saw a couple of similar picnic/camping sites. The only people we saw were a rider and passenger on a motor bike struggling up the steep mountain road.

Relieved at last, we reached the main mountain road, smooth surfaced rather than rocky and rutted. We had this mountain road to ourselves. As we rounded a tight corner suddenly the car swerved. It slid toward the edge of the road and teetered. I had shivers as I looked down at the steep drop below us. Sam reversed the car and we sat back to catch our breath. Having manoeuvred skillfully up through Cedar Valley, Sam was horrified that we had been so close to an accident on the main road. We got out to look at what had created the problem. Tiny particles of shale, almost like ball bearings had dropped down from the hillside scattering at that spot. The corner was shaded by a rocky overhang and this had disguised them. As Sam suggested we were probably so relieved after the long climb through the valley we had, as he said, '"Taken our eye off the ball".

We stopped to pull back the canvas roof on the car. It was wonderful to be alive and enjoy the bright sunlight and cool mountain breezes. The views were spectacular as we dropped down to Pomos as the Polis to Latchi coast was laid out before us.

Along the coast we found a busy and obviously popular seaside restaurant. I had the largest plate of fish and chips I have ever eaten. They were delicious!

Having driven along difficult paths, many of them isolated we had had some hair raising moments today. So much so, it felt as if we had been sailing!

Play Day

Wednesday August 22nd

Today we decided to put "Madonna" on the water for the first time. She is the inflatable tender from Triton.

Bought second hand, this was our inaugural sail. We laid her out on the pebbly beach along with her accessories which consisted of a couple of floor planks, a bench with a waterproof bag beneath, paddles and of course a foot pump and attachments. We took turns working the foot pump. It took time, patience and a lot of energy but eventually we got there. We fitted in the floor boards and bench seat and brought the hefty Honda 4 stroke 10 HP outboard motor from the Suzuki. Once the tender was in the water we fitted the outboard motor to Madonna's stern.

The sea was like glass. A perfect day! We headed north east around the Pissouri headland to Melanda Beach. Helming, Sam explained how the throttle and rudder worked. Whilst living in the UK he had owned a series of sport's boats. He confidently showed me how to control the ***throttle*** which accelerates or decelerates the boat. With a big grin he passed the throttle over to me. Having built up some confidence sailing the catamarans and Toppers here I was starting all over again. I felt overwhelmed with the certainly that I would get it all wrong.

My first impulse was to hand the throttle back, however reason took over as I knew this was a safety boat and I MUST learn how to use it. I could feel my heart pounding as my anxiety welled up. With a twist grip throttle, only the slightest movement was needed to rev it up. It felt as if I had been handed a stick of dynamite. I held it gingerly in my hand. My mind was flooded with doubts. Do I turn clockwise or anti-clockwise? How do I stop?

My first twist was jerky and we shot forward. However, I kept my nerve, settled myself and began to practice trying to use smaller increments until I built the speed up enough for the engine to purr as we slid across the water. I loved it. As I grew more confident I wanted to go a little faster. As I revved her up, Sam, delighted with my confidence, explained that the priority is economy. I must rev her back down to a steady purr and keep her there. I was doing fine. That was all that was needed.

I took Madonna as close to shore as I dared and then Sam took over. We had to pull her up onto the sand to beach her, so timing lifting the outboard motor inboard was essential.

We celebrated with a wonderful fish lunch and enjoyed the sunshine and a beer at the Melanda Beach Taverna.

As we motored back the wind began to pick up. This made progress slower as the bow of the boat was lifted by the building waves. The wind was now against us, catching the uplifted bow and trying to push us back. Sam took the helm, maintaining enough forward motion to keep us moving in the right direction. Slowly and steadily we made our way back.

Once Madonna and her motor were carefully stowed away we drove up the hill and put her safely on Sam's balcony.

At about 5pm we collected the catamaran equipment and set out in Kitty Moran, for a lovely, long evening sail. We had a little more wind than the morning, enough to fill her sails and take us out and round the headland. We sailed until the sun began to set and made our way back through a rose pink sea.

What a wonderful day! I knew I had passed another test.

A Sailor's Dream

Thursday August 23rd

I occasionally had work in Larnaca with my friend Marina. This provided a wonderful reason to have overnight stays on Triton moored at Larnaca Marina. However, midsummer meant it was getting hot, humid and less comfortable. Although Triton had air-conditioning in the cabins it was much more pleasant to create a natural breeze with strategically opened windows. However, the mosquitoes always seemed to find a way in and they were getting vicious.

Over the last months I had admired a 29 foot sail boat which was for sale. My friend Marina asked Sam if he would take a look. Her brother, based in the UK, was interested. Sam was very impressed she was set up for solo sailing with cassette main sails, all navigating equipment, safety equipment and much more. He asked if I was interested. I was astonished! It was such an enormous leap from 13 foot and 15 foot catamarans and dinghy's to a fully loaded ocean going sailboat. I was flattered. that Sam thought I might even consider such a thing!

I had a chat to Marina. She told me that her brother was interested in a number of boats and she suggested that I should go ahead and make an offer. Ecstatic, I made an arrangement to view the boat with the agent.

Sam suggested I should begin the negotiations myself and offered to support me during the next phase should it go further. The agent said there was someone interested; they had made an offer but that he would put my offer to the owner anyway.

I felt dizzy. Today was like moving through a dream. I kept pinching myself but did not wake up. I had not only stood on the boat of my dreams but by late afternoon was negotiating for it. It was incredible but also terrifying. Yet it had all taken place with such smoothness and flow it felt quite natural.

Tender Confidence

Saturday August 25th

Today the sea was perfectly still, glasslike. These were ideal conditions for motor boats. The smooth sea gave less resistance to the hull making the tender easy to manoeuver, resulting in using less fuel. We decided to take our second excursion on Madonna. To make inflating and assembling Madonna more fun we timed ourselves from parking the jeep and unloading all her parts to putting her in the water. It took us just over 20 minutes. It was much easier and quicker than before. Carrying the outboard motor down to the shore line took the most effort. It is heavy and cumbersome and Sam had to swing it up and over the back of the boat whilst I stood waist deep in the water and held her still.

We clambered aboard. Sam pulled on the rope start and the engine fired up. We were off! We had travelled about 100 metres when the engine spluttered to a stop. Oh dear! Sam unclipped the top of the engine cover and fiddled about within the workings. Satisfied that he had fixed the problem he tugged on the rope start, nothing. He tried again and again. He then opened up the engine cover once more and grimaced as he pulled out a broken cord, the rope start. This is essential for starting the motor. Without it we were going nowhere so we pulled out the oars, placed them in the rowlocks and rowed back. Undaunted Sam leapt into the Suzuki and dashed back to his place. He soon returned brandishing a fresh cord. He fitted it and off we went. Lucky for us it happened where it did. If we had stalled on our way to Melanda it would have been a long row back!

I helmed. Sam took over as we passed the headland. This was to be a training session. He demonstrated how important it was that I felt comfortable and in control. My wrist needed to be relaxed yet stable enough to hold the throttle position. He then gave a graphic demonstration of my taut wrist resulting in a jerky motion on the throttle. Madonna lurched, leap-frogging forward.

After wiping away my tears of laughter I felt much more relaxed and confident as I took the helm.

The main objective Sam set for me today is to operate Madonna at the most economical, functional and comfortable level possible. It is a fine balance but well worth mastering.

Sam's aim was to have Madonna available to use as a rescue boat when we are sailing. It would mean, with Sam in the Madonna or visa-versa we could go solo for longer sails in the Wave. We could sail on days when the wind is forecast to drop, knowing we have the option of towing the boat in with Madonna. This would be a huge bonus as we could enjoy more sailing days. We could even travel further and be more adventurous. Would I be up to the task?

Our training concluded with lunch at Melanda a perfect opportunity to debrief over a beer. Sam reassured me, making it clear I was making good progress. After our debrief Sam told me he would be flying to the UK on Sunday evening. He will be in the UK for 10 days. He is returning for a family wedding. It was a last minute decision.

I helmed back. It was uneventful. With my enthusiasm at its peak I felt very disappointed that we would have such a long break.

I will miss my sailing. I will really miss Sam.

Sinking Sensation

Friday September 7th

To celebrate Sam's return we decided to go for a gentle evening sail on "Kitty Moran". There was just enough wind for us to maneuver her in Pissouri Bay.

Having had an enforced two week break, I was sure I would have far less problems with my rib. I was devastated that once back on the water it was as painful as ever. In fact it was worse; so painful that I could not even help with the launch today.

I felt miserable and decided not to sail. Realizing my discomfort, Sam insisted I join him and suggested I sit by the mast in the centre of the boat. It seemed a good idea as it would minimize my upper body movement and therefore the potential for pain would be reduced.

It felt really odd being a passenger rather than crew. Nothing was expected of me. As the wind picked up a little, Sam drew the mainsheet in tightly to sail close haul. With the wind blowing through my hair and the salt water on my face I began to feel alive again. I felt much more positive, enjoying the sense of freedom and excitement as we skimmed across the water. Leaning against the mast I was able to look aft and leisurely enjoy the view from a rarely glimpsed angle. As crew, my role is to focus forward keeping a lookout for hazards.. When helming I would occasionally glance aft over my shoulder to look out for oncoming boats and back towards land to monitor how far out we had sailed.

We headed south east, Sam tacked to take us beyond Black Rock, and then with his usual confident ease he gybed. As he completed the turn, the windward bow began to sink. Horrified, I clawed at the decking as I was being swept underwater. Both bows were submerged. With my finger wrapped firmly around the decking chord I hauled myself up out of the water. Swiftly I moved aft and braced myself against Sam. Seconds later the bows lifted

70

out of the nose-dive and the boat righted. We were off once again. This time I stayed safely next to Sam.

During our debrief we laughed helplessly as we each recounted our version of the sail. The boat's behavior, although unexpected, made sense. Usually as we prepare to gybe I am crouched tightly in the center of the boat, looking towards the mast, ready to spring to the windward side to balance the boat. Today I had been leaning against the mast, totally relaxed. My weight was too far forward for the manoeuver and the boat responded correctly. The nose-dive was inevitable. Had we been sailing on the Hobie 15 we would have "pitch poled": this is when the catamaran goes into a forward summersault. This is to be avoided at all costs as it can result in injured crew and a damaged boat. At the very least the crew would be badly shaken.

Sam often described the Wave as a Land Rover: strong, sturdy and nigh on impossible to capsize. It was time to re-evaluate. The Wave was much more sensitive than first thought.

Tender Practice

Saturday September 8th

Today we had such beautiful soft seas that we decided to take Madonna, to Melanda once again. The conditions were perfect for practice.

Sam instructed me to helm all the way there and promised that, depending on my progress, I could helm all the way back. I felt myself relax as I helmed. Confidently, I began to experiment gently adjusting the throttle and shifting our direction with the rudder. It felt wonderful. I made the most of the opportunity to fine-tune my hand position and tweak the speed until I felt the comfortable gentle purr of the engine which indicated the best, economical use of fuel.

Sam lay across the boat sunbathing with his legs over the side. With his eyes closed he had a look of sheer serenity and absolute trust. It was a perfect acknowledgement that the gentle purring of the motor in my command was just as it should be.

As we approached the shore at Melanda Beach, Sam took over. He demonstrated how to tilt the outboard engine towards the boat so that the propellers come out of the water. It is a time sensitive manoeuvre. You need sufficient power to get to shore but once in the shallows the propellers can be damaged if prompt action is not taken. Sam promised me some land practice over the next few weeks.

Solo Confidence

Sunday September 9th

Today Sam and I had a leisurely Sunday swim across Pissouri Bay. I love swimming in the sea. Before I began learning to sail, for years I swam at least five days a week from April to October. My idea of heaven was to swim for an hour or more and then sit on the beach to eat my homemade breakfast of muesli in a jar with rice milk or to savor marmite on toast with a flask of tea

This year sailing, reading about sailing, thinking about sailing and watching sailing videos on YouTube, not to mention searching the internet for boat parts needed for repairs, had taken up so much of my time that I have hardly been swimming at all.

With breakfast over we gathered up our sailing and personal equipment and set off for Pissouri Bay once more. It was a perfect day to sail the Toppers.

Toppers are very popular with sailing clubs. They are usually kept on beach trailers. Once rigged the Topper is simply wheeled into the water by the beach crew. It is then floated off the trailer and the sailor clambers in and sails away.

We do not have a trailer fit for the toppers yet so we carry them down to the water's edge one by one where we rig them.

The Toppers are kept as far away from the water as possible, otherwise at high tide they would float away. They sit nestled beside three young Eucalyptus trees and an old fishing boat. To carry them from their resting place onto the water had become much easier thanks to my exercise regime.

At the bow of the Topper is a rope known as a ***painter***, a sailing term for a rope which can be used to tow or restrain a boat. Sam has fitted a toggle to the painter to create a mini carrying handle. As the stern is wider and heavier it needs to be carried, requiring significant arm strength and very strong finger tips. Thankfully, Sam carries the stern most of the time. I take the bow holding onto the toggle. Even though we are both fit, it is still a struggle slipping and sliding over the rocks and down the shingly slope. The boats often swing on the rope resulting in my having bruised and battered shins.

Thankfully as I am capsizing less, the odd body bruises I get when I do, have time to recover. There was a time during mid summer when I had to constantly wear long sleeved shirts and trousers. This was not just for cosmetic reasons. I had so many bruises of varying hues it looked as if I was being regularly battered. As Sam and I spent so much time together, he would be seen as the obvious assailant. I did not want him arrested for assault!

Today, once I launched Vitamin C, I leapt aboard with a rush of confidence. Having learnt the basics of sailing I am getting a clearer picture of where I am going and how to get to where I want to be. Sailing solo gives me the opportunity to make my own mistakes and try and puzzle out the solutions. I love learning with Sam as he drives me forward, challenging me with his training and teaching techniques.

Sailing solo gives me an opportunity to indulge myself. I can slow down the learning pace to my own comfort zone so that I can think my way through the, as yet, unsolved mysteries. I was eager to get started.

Today's challenge, which I set myself, is to make as many clean transitions as I can when I tack, sweeping across the "no-go zone" as I turn the boat. Sometimes, try as I might, the boom (a pole fixed along the bottom edge of the sail that improves the angle and shape of the sail) simply sits there and does not swing over to the other side of the boat as I tack. As a result not only have I not turned but the boat ends up becalmed in a lye-to position on the edge of the "no-go zone" or even in irons stuck in the "no-go zone".

Sam has demonstrated how to grasp hold of the boom and push it across, whilst at the same time pushing the tiller in the same direction. This particularly helps when I am in irons as it puts the boat into reverse, turning away from the wind as I *back the mainsail.* In order to do this I need to pull the boom towards me as I pull the rudder, enabling her to find the wind once more. This technique is called 'push, push/pull, pull" in the RYA books. Sam makes it look so easy.

Why do I find it so difficult?

During today's practice I have come to the conclusion that perhaps I may not be building up enough speed before I begin to turn the boat. Being over cautious, I might be navigating the turn too slowly. I must experiment some more.

Coming Together

Tuesday September 11th

It was quite some time since we sailed the Hobie 15 in Limassol. Today is such a perfect day; we quickly loaded the Suzuki and dashed down to Limassol.

Georgiou at West Winds welcomed us with his usual beaming smile. He was delighted and perhaps a little surprised that I had persevered with my sailing. As his water sports centre caters mainly for holiday makers many of his customers approach sailing as holiday activity or it's a passing phase. Sailing a catamaran is a very wet sport. Not every ones idea of a good time. Especially in September as the water is already much cooler.

We rigged Sam's Kitten Kat in record time. Sam helmed as we took her out through the little harbor and then we flew. The conditions were fantastic! The wind was blowing SW onshore off a SSE facing coastline. We switched as crew and helm a number of times with me taking the helm at every opportunity. Under Sam's watchful eye I performed a number of manoeuvres. I paid particular attention to how much I adjusted the mainsheet for each turn, making sure that I tighten her a little for a gybe, so that there is less movement as the sail swings across. Ideally during a gybe one also needs to hold onto the upper mainsheet to perform a **controlled assist**. Literally by holding onto the upper mainsheet you are slowing the movement of the sail, assisting it as it moves across, rather than having it snap across with great force. This can injure the helm and create great strain on the sail and fittings.

In certain strong sea and wind conditions when trying to tack the boat the bow will refuse to go through the strong wind and strong seas – it stalls in the "no-go zone". This can be due to a slow initial turning speed while heading into the wind. Due to stalling, the lack of water flow over the rudder will cause the sailor to lose the ability to steer the boat. The boat is in irons, unable to move, rather like a person being manacled.

In these extreme conditions we use a procedure which Sam refers to as "coming fully about". This requires the bow of the boat to fall away from the wind, rather than turning through it. This brings the stern through the wind to perform a gybe. Then still moving in the same direction, the bows come back into the wind on the opposite side of the "no-go zone". In doing so the boat has turned about 300 degrees. During this manoeuver the sail can swing with great velocity across the deck jerking the boat and crew, violently. Sheeting in and performing a control assist (holding the sail to guide it across) can greatly reduce this.

When tacking, the mainsail is, usually, already very tight on close haul. As the bow moves only 60 degrees plus or minus across the "no-go zone", heading into the wind, I release the sail a little, allowing it more movement as it swings across in order to bring the catamaran around, ready to adjust the jib sail. The correct use of the jib helps the boat to bear away to leeward thus avoiding the "no-go zone".

There are always sailing conditions where you have to break your own rules and do the opposite to the norm. For example, the wind direction can suddenly change by as much as 180 degrees, a phenomena quite frequent in Pissouri Bay. The practice today has helped me to be more prepared for such eventualities. Through deepening my understanding of what is happening I can better react in emergencies.

In the Hobie 15, leaning over the stern and reclaiming the tiller extension after turning is still a painful movement for me. It triggers my rib, drawing my attention away from the mainsheet and manoeuvring of the rudders. The only way to overcome this appears to be to practise and practise until it become automatic.

Over and over again, I tossed the rudder bar over the stern, turned the rudders with the rudder bar and ducked around the mainsail to sit on the other hull. I faced aft as I work with the rudder and forward as I adjusted the mainsheet, whilst setting the next point of sail. It felt much easier by the end of the day.

The intense practice in Pissouri Bay has made an enormous difference to my confidence in sailing the Hobie 15 in Limassol. I can see and feel the vast improvements I have made. As I look back I can remember my initial terror of the first sail on the Hobie 15. It was only 4 months ago!

I am beginning to feel like a sailor and it feels wonderful.

Calm Toppers

Wednesday September 12th

With my enthusiasm running high I persuaded Sam to sail again today. We went down to Pissouri Bay where the wind was gusting Force 2, enough to sail the Toppers but not the Wave.

In unison, Sam and I had the boats rigged and ready to sail. As the boats slid out smoothly past the rocks and slipped through the water, I thought back to the many launchings where I had been bumped and jostled as the Toppers were swung around by the shifting wind and choppy seas, often leading to a capsize before even climbing aboard.

I remembered the bruised shins and hips not to mention the grit and determination it took for me to get the boat afloat and away from the beach on days when it seemed impossible. On those days I was often driven by self talk. I talked myself through the procedures over and over again until the Topper was facing the right direction and then when the wind picked up the sail filled and I was off. What a glorious sense of achievement it gave me! The greater the struggle in those early days, the better it felt to be out there.

Many of the challenges related to our location. We had to keep the Toppers out of the swimming area to the left which was covetously guarded by the Colombia Beach Resort. This was the most exclusive section of their Pissouri Hotel complex. In addition, we had to avoid swimmers who had nonchalantly swum into the boat lane, totally unaware of the damage an inexperienced sailor can inflict. To the left were power boats and occasionally yachts, many of which belonged to residents of the Hotel and Resort, on sea moorings. These were very expensive and it was essential to navigate around them rather than sail into them. It was not an ideal location for a beginner but easy access to the beach was a major compensation.

As we navigated our way through to the less congested center of the bay the winds dropped to a mere whisper and the sea state shifted to soft, almost still. Determined, I meandered around for a while trying to practice figures of eight needed for man overboard rescue but it was impossible to turn. You have to have wind motion to navigate.

Unable to complete any figures of eight, I ended up going round in circles for a while identifying the different points of sail and adjusting my sail and 'dagger board', a central fin, which is lifted and lowered from inside the boat. When sailing close haul the sail is 45 degrees from the wind and the dagger board needs lowered to balance the pull of the sail. On a broad reach, with the sail at 90° from the wind, the dagger board is halfway up and on a run when there is little sail pressure; it is as high as possible without catching on the boom.

I could see Sam further out toward the headland, lying across the width of his boat, sunbathing. He was chilling out waiting for the winds to return. However they did not. Very slowly, disappointed, independently we made our way back to shore.

I find the calm seas very frustrating. The motion of the boat is languid, and even in the light Toppers it is very difficult to steer and change the directions of sail. Reading the RYA books in my own time and linking the information with all that Sam has taught me has given me a broader understanding. My knowledge is deepening and I feel a keen, inexplicable sense of urgency to try out all that I am learning.

Becalmed

Thursday September 13th

The calm seas have stayed with us. I pressured Sam to sail today as I am eager to catch up on my sailing time. Our roles have reversed it would seem, as it was originally Sam who wanted to sail in all conditions. Perhaps becoming more independent in my sailing, more of a sailing companion than a student is enabling Sam to relax more. However this has not dulled MY enthusiasm. Just the opposite!

With a good wind and calm seas we would be able to sail at maximum speed without being challenged by the waves. However, today was tedious. We had just enough wind to get us out into the bay and once there, we floundered about. It was very difficult and frustrating trying to navigate the boat for once again the wind dropped. It took us over 40 minutes to get back to shore. This was only managed by patiently waiting to pick up occasional puffs of wind and then making the most of them.

As catamarans have two hulls and a deck connecting them they are not streamlined in the same way a yacht or sailboat is. The beauty of a catamaran is that when sailing **close hauled** (tight to the wind), the windward hull, the one you are sitting on, lifts out of the water gently kissing it. Then the boat is really streamlined. You are then sitting on the raised hull with your feet in the toe straps, leaning right out over the side to balance the boat. The main objective is to ensure that the hull in the water does not get buried in the waves. In more advanced sailing one or both crew members would be out hooked onto a trapeze wire, which is attached to the mast. With only their feet on the hull they can lean right out over the water shifting and changing body position and moving up and down the hull to balance the boat. It looks very exciting, requiring skillful management.

When tacking, as you switch over from one hull to the other, both hulls must be in the water. It is essential to have the wind speed to provide the acceleration to swing the boat round through the wind and into a tack.

At times it is imperative to tack for the safety of the boat and crew. In Pissouri Bay we have headlands, cliffs and underwater rocks which must be avoided. Wind speed is essential in order to navigate around them. In addition the wind sweeps down a steep valley and creates turbulence after which there is calm water and no wind, a dead spot. You can be sailing at speed then suddenly you meet a dead spot. Quick thinking and immediate action are required as you navigate the boat's stall as it goes into irons and then wait for the wind to pick up as you pass through the dead spot.

Hanging Out

Friday September 14th

Thank goodness we had a change in the weather today. To celebrate we dashed over to Limassol to sail the Hobie 15. As we drove along the highway, which runs parallel to the coast, many of the waves had white caps which were clearly visible indicating a Force 4 plus. My stomach knotted with a mixture of anticipation and dread. The impatient gusting wind was buffeting Sam's Suzuki, as if telling us to hurry along and get into the water.

Having had the two calm days we were determined to sail. To maximize our time, Georgiou insisted we take one of his ready rigged Hobie 15's, as in these wild conditions he did not expect us to be out there for long. We had already noted that there were very few boats on the water.

As Sam guided the catamaran out of the lagoon, we were hit by the gusting winds and the sharply contrasting sea states. Once beyond the sea wall within seconds we met two metre waves. The wind took my breath away. Sam tacked. We were off at roaring pace! Ahead of us a large **RIB** (rigid inflatable boat) , similar to but larger than Madonna, was zooming along. Suddenly the wind caught it. It tipped right over onto its edge, and then teetered at almost 90 degrees, the helm desperately held on, the engine whirring. We gasped in horror. The boat seemed to be suspended in time and space. With a great splash, the boat's hull hit the water and he was roaring off once more.

We were racing towards the same spot at alarming speed. We were there within moments. I held my breath and thrust my feet deep into the foot straps. I hooked my feet in whilst lacing my fingers into the webbing. I clutched onto the trampoline tightly. Within seconds we were flung up in the air. Our hull went straight up in the air. Sam was hanging on. I leaned back over the hull. My upper body was right over the edge. I could feel my muscles taut with maximum extension. We were still sailing! Rather than being afraid, I found it incredibly exciting. I held on.

With a resounding bang she hit the water. Incredibly, Sam had managed to reach down and kick release the mainsail sheet. The sail, our engine, flapped loosely above us as if too were exhausted. Sam turned and grinned at me. Still breathless, he managed to mouth "Well done!"

We had been a couple of degrees off what would have been a very dangerous capsize.

With the wind a little calmer, we looked landward. It was clear to see how the wind had hurtled down a steep valley coming out onto the coast like a fist ready to punch out at anything that got in its way. Greatly relieved and still much shaken we sailed on.

Sam told me later how impressed he had been by my cool action. Had I panicked, we would certainly have capsized. A capsize in those conditions meant at the very least, she could have rolled over and over or even cart wheeled in any direction. It such high winds and challenging sea conditions it would also have been really tricky to right her.

We were greatly relieved to get back to land, relatively dry and safe. I was deeply satisfied that I had passed an important test. I was rapidly becoming the crew member that Sam could trust in emergencies. Not just his student. Most importantly for me this had been a natural transition. Not forced. I had done what I had done without any prompting but because it felt right to do so.

This incident seeded in me a burning desire to use a harness. The harness is worn under or over your lifejacket. It has a front hook which is located between your chest and navel. The hook is then attached to the attachment on the wire. The wire and attachment is called a trapeze. It is rightly named, for just like the circus trapeze, once attach to it your weight is completely supported. With poise, you can you lean right out of the boat backwards and side-step along the hull. It is a very effective method of trimming and balancing the boat in high winds and difficult conditions. I felt ready, as crew, to take this next step and use a harness. It would enable us to sail further and faster as we could go out in higher winds, just like today.

Sam was still uncertain. He felt a responsibility for my safety. The chances of my being injured whilst using a harness he knew were much, much greater. He made it clear we would be sailing much faster therefore the chances of a major accident would be greatly increased. Even with a slight misjudgment such as suddenly loosing the wind whilst he was helming could lead to me being flung around or into the mast and stanchions (which are part of the standing rigging) holding up the mast.

When we first started to sail together Sam did not believe I would ever get to this stage. Weighing in at just 70 kg himself, he had believed that to maximize Sam's Kitten Cat's performance he would have needed a heavier crew member to stabilize the boat. He had made it quite clear he was not willing to make the financial investment for two harnesses. However, what had started off as a bit of fun, a way to pass the summertime, was becoming a passion for me. I was growing to love the speed and excitement of the Hobie 15.

Changing Roles

Sam had a house guest, his friend Paul from the UK, a fellow snow-skier known as "Moose". Moose had sailed with Sam before.

It was a great day for a sail, with a SW wind gusting from Force 3 to 4. Sam decided we would sail in Pissouri Bay. With Moose and I on the Wave, he would go out on his Topper, Blue Tac.

It was blustery with the wind building as we helped Sam move the Topper onto the beach. Moose and I then headed back to rig the Wave. Sam was sailing ahead of us as we set sail from Yannos's Water Sports. Suddenly he capsized. It was his first capsize in a Topper. He told us later that before he came about he was on close haul. As he was about to tack he quickly released his mainsheet allowing his sail enough slack to flick over and make an easy transition across the boat. Right at that moment, a gust of wind caught the sail, the boat heeled and with the mainsheet loosened the boom touched the water and over he went. I have made similar mistakes in the past but through tacking so slowly that as I moved through, the wind flicked the boom across and took me unawares. Startled I upset the boat balance and capsized.

With Moose helming the Wave we sailed over to see if we could assist. Sam waved us away. As we tacked I could see him swimming the upturned Topper into the wind to make her more stable once she was righted. She was pointing into the wind, the no-go area; therefore her sails would not catch the wind and blow the boat over again which is always a risk as you scramble over the side. I began to appreciate my own struggles watching him. I had lost count how many times I had capsized. I had certainly had lots of practice!

I began to run through the procedure in my mind. The first thing is hold onto the boat by keeping a tight grip on the mainsheet. If it is trapped around the rudders or the rudder extension it must be untangled. Then, firmly holding onto the mainsheet, the next step is to check that the rudder and the dagger board are securely in place and adjust where necessary. The next step is to swim around to the hull side and whilst holding onto the main sheet pull yourself up onto the dagger board, lean across it and bounce your weight until the sails begin to lift up out of the water and the hull sinks back onto the water. An additional challenge is that when the sail is full of water the mast may be also. This adds quite a few kilograms to the sail and slows the process. Once the sail and mast are freed from the grasp of the sea the hull can come down heavily. You must move back quickly to avoid it.

Sam had soon clambered aboard the righted Topper and together we sailed out toward Cape Aspro.

The wind was gusting Force 4. We were flying along on the Wave. All of a sudden, as Moose gybed, there was an ear-cracking snap and the large metal clip which attached the clew at the end of the mainsail and the main outhaul (made up of a series of pulleys which control the mainsheet) snapped and flew off. With the sail flapping freely we had absolutely no sail power! The Wave does not have a jib sail. I grabbed hold of the flapping mainsail sail and pushed my fingers through the hole and held on. Ouch! I quickly learnt more than I wanted to know about the power of the wind that day.

The greatest force on the sail is at the clew, as this is where the mainsheet runs through the outhaul to mainsail. The mainsheet, which is a rope, acts rather like a fishing line when playing the fish, the sail being the fish. The clew is where the fish hook would be. My fingers were holding the sail and mainsheet together in the same way as the fish hook. It was excruciatingly exhausting!

Moose and I change places a number of times. I took the helm when Moose hung onto the sail. Although Moose had considerably more strength that I, his hands and fingers were much bigger than mine, so that it was with brute force and sheer determination that he held on.

We gradually made our way into shore. With our energies spent, the sea state began to shift creating a swell which played with the Wave and floated us in.

Sam had been totally unaware of our plight. He had been zipping back and forth on the Topper. We did not know it but he had a spare clip in his pocket. Even if we had known he was too far away for us to communicate. We had talked about having mobile phones in waterproof bags with us as we sail. It is time to take this a step further.

It was another important lesson for me on how a simple failure on a boat could have dire consequences. Each hook and clip is there for a purpose. When learning to sail it is vital to know the role of each, for at least then when something goes wrong you can try and find a temporary solution to get you home.

Safety First

With Moose's holiday over Sam and I are back into our sailing routine once more but with some additional safety precautions.

Sam is still annoyed with himself for Thursday's equipment failure. I am still rather shaken. If either of us had been sailing solo, it would have been quite terrifying. There had been nothing on the boat to tie through the clew of the sail and connect the mainsheet or even simply hold onto it. I could not have held onto the sail for more than a few minutes at a time and whilst doing so I would not have been able to reach the rudder bar as we do not have a rudder extension on the Wave. Luckily there had been two of us. Moose had been quite happy to be the hero of the day.

Without a sail you are at the mercy of the sea. We had been near to the rocky headland when the clip had snapped. The catamaran could have been rammed up against the rocks and there would have been nothing I could have done about that.

Sam now rightly insists that before we sail, whenever we sail, we run a check on all the clips and attachments to make sure everything is in good order and secure. The broken clip has been replaced and an emergency clip stowed away along with a long piece of emergency rope. This experience and new regime is helping me to gain a realistic knowledge of ongoing boat maintenance. Up to this point Sam has taken the full responsibility for boat maintenance. He enjoys it and as we are sailing his boats he has felt it to be his responsibility. I had wanted to be more involved for some time and now I am eager to learn more knowing this will stand me in good stead for future sailing.

We had already replaced all the galvanized boat clips on the Toppers and the Wave with stainless steel ones. As the Hobie 15 is only one year old, all her fittings are stainless steel originals and don't need replacing. We will however keep an eye on wear and tear. Sam has followed a regular routine check of pins and attachments which can work loose due to the movement of the boat. Now with two sets of eyes we can be even more vigilant. Even then, something can always take us by surprise as it did last Thursday.

The more aware you become, the more responsibility there is to prepare for an ever-widening range of eventualities. In addition to dealing with the randomness of the wind, sea and weather, I am discovering that sailing requires detailed observation of all the boat parts under strain and dealing with the maintenance, repair and replacement of aging boat parts. New parts also need to be examined regularly as they are not always suitable and are sometimes poorly made.

I appreciate that Sam is so vigilant. To begin with I interpreted his carefulness as over-care even fussiness. I wanted to be out on the water sailing not fiddling with a clip which is not as tight as it should be or tightening the wrap around the Toppers tiller extension so it does not flap around too much. I am learning to sail safely and anticipate problems and to be flexible enough to try out options, even if they seem a little crazy at the time. An example of this is the clever solution Sam found to ensure the rudder on Vitamin C remains fixed in place. When I used the tiller extension in some positions it acted as a lever, lifting the spigot (small peg on the tiller) out of the rudder mounting. The rudder would then fall off into the water. I would then have to quickly clamber over the side of the boat to reclaim it. Whilst swimming in the sea and holding onto the boat it was a struggle to reattach the rudder. Sam's solution was to drill a small hole through the spigot and attached a fixing pin which kept the tiller in place. It was fiddly to put on but served its purpose perfectly and saved me so much frustration.

The problems which are encountered all go into a treasure box of solutions for future possibilities. The more I sail, the more I learn and the more confident I become. I am really grateful to have these opportunities to sail Sam's boats.

After today's boat check we have the Wave rigged and on the water in no time. The wind was blowing a gentle Force 2 to 3 which offered a perfect opportunity for me to take the helm. Eager to do so, I launched her and helmed the whole journey. I was thrilled that at the end of our sail that I was able to bring her through the boat lane and to shore without any direction from

Sam. Sam sat happily throughout, enjoying the sail. He tells me he is confident I am ready to sail the Wave solo, but he is not pushing me.

I find I learn most efficiently when I can take something I have learnt and reapply it to something else in my life. It reinforces and deepens the lesson making it a multi-sensory, organic learning process. Sailing the Hobie 15, Hobie Wave and Topper, three very different types of boats, offers me the perfect opportunity to do this. The Hobie 15 is a racing boat, fast and furious and very sensitive to handling. The Hobie 13 is steady and reliable, slower to respond but very stable in most weather conditions. The Toppers are light, fun, fast and very tippy. At this time I feel that I am still in the midst of confidence building, information gathering and investigatory processes on all three boats. I am happy sailing solo in the Topper but I don't feel I am quite ready to apply my learning to sail solo in the Hobies YET. After all I have not yet experienced a capsize on either catamaran nor learnt how to right one.

Breaking Barriers

Thursday 27th September

We sailed the Toppers out of the safety of Pissouri Bay into the deeper, less protected coastal waters. It was a great moment for me to confidently sail past Black Rock. I felt a shiver of excitement as I looked back and felt in awe of my new found confidence.

Beyond Black Rock, the escarpment runs down almost directly into the sea. The sheer-faced cliffs are fluted from erosion, rather like enormous organ pipes. The rock formations with their stunning striations glow golden with the reflected sunlight.

A narrow sandy path runs along the bottom of the cliffs, exposed only when the tide is low. I have heard it said that the Mediterranean is not tidal but the shifting sands and constantly changing beaches of Pissouri Bay and around the island seem to prove otherwise.

Heading out towards the yellow buoy today is yet another landmark moment. It is a deep sea marker for passing ships, clearly visible even from my home at the top of Pissouri Hill, fifteen minutes drive from the beach. It is clear evidence that we are definitely away from the safety of the bay. For weeks now it seems to have become bigger and brighter, luring me from the bay to visit it.

As we rounded the headland my sail flicked around taut and tight as the wind picked up. The choppy sea buffeted Vitamin C's hull lifting her up and dashing her into the oncoming waves. I already had my feet hooked underneath the foot straps. In these conditions it was vital to lean right out, over the edge of the boat to maintain boat balance. As her bow lifted above the wave and dived into the trough I had to constantly trim the boat by sliding along, shifting my position from bow to stern depending on which stage of the wave I was sailing. Keeping the sail taught in close-haul became more and more challenging. The mainsheet viciously tugged and pulled digging into my hand, demanding all my strength.

Sam had instilled in me that close-haul was the safest aspect to sail in under these conditions. Being closest to the wind, it is the fastest aspect not just in speed but in distance covered. If you have set the correct point of sail and stick to it you will get there sooner. The speed generated enables greater boat control and ease of manoeuvres.

Time and time again the boat heeled almost to the point of capsize, at which critical point I would release the sail a little and shift into a close reach, a little further from the wind. It was incredibly exhilarating. The mainsheet feels like the tightly stretched reigns of my horse Nousa, as we galloped swiftly through the desert. As the hull lifts and my feet dig into the foot-straps, I remember the thrill as I leaned forward, bringing my weight into the stirrups, poised in space, whispering in her ear. Nousa's stride lengthened and became smoother, oiled by motion. No longer horse and rider we were one. Now, I too am one with the boat.

It was vital that the boom did not touch the water, for at these speeds a capsize would be instant and dangerous. The choppy sea conditions would make righting the Topper very difficult as the waves would keep turning her away from the desired "no-go zone". Once righted the wind would catch the sail and she would be flicked over again. Ideally I should have loosened the kicking strap, a cleated rope attachment, on the boom which is connected to the mast. It is used to control the lift of the boom and the mainsail twist in high winds is a means to de-power. In order to do so I would have to bring the boat into the wind and lye-to. As you are facing into the wind the wind cannot fill the sails. This is the closest to stopping you can achieve whilst sailing. However, if I lye-to, I would momentarily go head to wind close to 'irons' and would lose the speed which I had built up. As there is no boat movement and therefore no power it can be a tricky position to move out of. I could end up floundering. This would have created even more distance between Sam and I. He is clearly visible ahead of me, sailing Blue Tac. I did not want to lose sight of him. I did not want to be out there alone.

I coiled the mainsheet around my hand a few more times, wincing as the rope dug deeper through my glove and chaffed my hands. With my feet tucked deeper into the foot straps, I tenuously leaned even further out over the side of the heeling boat, ignoring my stomach muscles which ached with tension and stress. I was right on the edge, the sharp edge of the gunnels were digging into my buttocks. I clenched my teeth with the effort. With my stomach churning with anxiety, drawing on all my courage and determination I held on. My galloping steed was becoming a bucking bronco.

I was frustrated to the point of tears, for try as I might, I could not follow Sam's line of sail. He was sailing further away from me by the minute. This was because I had to keep releasing the sail a little to relieve the pressure on my hand, as well as to control the heeling of the boat. This meant that I was moving from close haul to close-reach and back to close-haul again and again. I was sailing in a zigzag, therefore having to sail a greater distance and he was sailing a direct straight line.

Later during our debrief Sam explained that in addition I had not been allowing for the drag of the water on the dagger board. The dagger board slides up and down like a dagger in a sheath. On bigger boats the dagger board is on a pivot and is called a centre board. When sailing windward or into the wind, the dagger board needs to be fully down. This is the strongest point of sail. The drag of the water on the dagger board balances the opposite sideways pull of the wind on the sail creating a lateral resistance to reduce leeway and helps you sail more efficiently to reach your point of destination. This balances the boat therefore increasing the forward momentum. When sailing *leeward*, the point of sail when the wind is behind you, on a *run*, the dagger board needs to be up, as the winds push on the sail is reduced so the pull on the dagger board also needs to be reduced to keep the boat upright.

I had been concentrating so hard on keeping the Topper upright and trying to follow Sam's trail that it seemed to take forever to reach the yellow buoy. Suddenly there it was. I almost sailed past it! The seagulls sitting on the buoy shared my excitement, squealing with delight as I tacked, sailed by the buoy, then I reached out to pat it in thanks as I passed. Ecstatic, with a huge grin I brought my Topper to sit beside Sam's. He too looked exhausted and was clearly as elated, beaming from ear to ear. It was a wonderful moment.

From the yellow buoy we could see a chain of bays stretch ahead of us along the coast. The closest, Melanda Beach and

Curium Beach were clearly within reach. The dream of destination sailing ceased to be a dream at that moment. More than a possibility, it was a certainty. I felt the buzz of anticipation. Invigorated, I felt myself expand. At that moment everything seemed possible.

My eyes glowed with anticipation of the adventures to come. I was brought back to reality as my aching body, buzzed and throbbed with the physical strain and effort of the sail. Reaching the yellow buoy was truly a significant milestone. Sailing through the most turbulent waters I have sailed to this point on the Topper, I felt the adrenaline coursing through my veins. Even my brain was exhausted. I did not know whether to laugh or cry.

We still had to sail back of course. However, the return journey would be psychologically different. From the start point of the yellow buoy Pissouri Bay would be in sight. I just had to keep sailing in that direction as I tacked back.

I marveled that I had achieved what was for me the greatest challenge of the day. I had solo sailed directly out to sea, leaving the safety of the coast behind.

Motivation

Saturday 29th September

With the carrot of sailing to Melanda Bay dangling before us, tempting us to further stretch our skills, our sailing program was radically revised. The plan was to follow a daily exercise program, extend our daily sailing and build up our sailing muscles. Whilst building up our strength and stamina, we would also be establishing a clearer picture of the resilience of the Toppers in sea conditions.

Toppers are small, one man sailing boats. They are usually sailed on lakes and reservoirs. We could be subjecting them to a severe beating by taking them out to sea. Were they up to it? The hulls which are made of composite plastic were strong but Vitamin C takes water in directly into the hull when we are in rough seas. This makes her harder to manoeuvre. How much wind pressure could the masts take? Our one luxury is that we have water bottle holders attached to the hull. This makes it easy to grab a sip of water. It is essential to keep hydrated whilst sailing. There are so many what ifs. One of the most crucial is: What would we do if one of the sails ripped. The Toppers have no storage space for spares. I take my waterproof stuff bag. It is a great design which self seals when rolled down on itself. It is then clipped to the bottom of the mast. It takes a spare water bottle and a throw-on top for when we pop into a restaurant. When I find a reliable waterproof case, it will take my mobile phone too. I certainly could not fit a spare sail in there!

The most challenging aspect of Topper sailing is that they capsize easily. Our masts seem to take in water, even though we have used new masts bungs to override this. This makes the water-filled sail even heavier to pull up out of the water. We would not knowingly sail the Toppers in challenging conditions but coastal weather can rapidly change. Righting a Topper in the sea with cresting waves is both difficult and dangerous. It is arduous swimming the boat round in order to turn her bow into the wind. It is almost impossible to keep her there as you clamber aboard. As the wind catches the sail, the movement of the waves spins her round until she is back to where you began. The greatest danger is she can capsize again, immediately. The toil of righting her is totally exhausting. Worst of all, especially with a water logged mast she can **turn turtle.** This is when the boat turns right over. She lays hull upwards in the water with the mast and sail below the boat. The dagger board can easily slip through its slot and out of the hull. It then has to be reinserted by swimming beneath the boat and jammed to stop it slipping out again, before righting the boat can even begin. It is essential to have the dagger board in place as leaning or bouncing ones weight on it provides the pivotal motion to bring the boat to her side and where she can be righted.

Sailing to a destination and back was my definition of REAL sailing. Solo sailing the Topper is helping me to make the shift from learning HOW to sail, to REALLY sailing. It was an incredible opportunity to test my sailing skills and seamanship. Could I get the best out of my boat? Did I feel up to the challenge?

I was keen to give it my best.

To reach Melanda Bay we would first have to sail out to the yellow buoy, the journey we had undertaken last Thursday. From there, we had to sail almost the same distance again into Melanda Bay. It had taken all of my strength and courage to sail out to the buoy only a few days before.

I felt exquisitely motivated by the thrill of adventure. I needed to develop greater confidence but more than that, I needed the grit, determination and drive to see each sailing project through. Neither of us would be able to 'bail out' easily if we got into trouble.

Today's sail felt radically different in every way. We sailed further out of Pissouri Bay to get used to the higher waves. They rolled us, toying with us playfully with the swell rocking the boats from side to side. Ahead of me every now and then Sam would disappear as he and his boat were caught in a deep trough. Within seconds she would bob up surfing the top of the wave. The wind was cooler and sharper as we were no longer protected by the bay. More clothing layers would be needed next time.

Today's sail felt radically different in every way. We sailed further out of Pissouri Bay than we had done before to get used to the higher waves. They rolled us, toying with us playfully with the swell rocking the boats from side to side. Ahead of me every now and then Sam would disappear as he and his boat were caught in a deep trough. Within seconds she would bob up surfing the top of the wave. The wind was cooler and sharper as we were no longer protected by the bay. More clothing layers would be needed next time.

We kept moving to keep warm and to push ourselves towards sailing longer distances. We sailed well within sight of each other so that if one of us had a problem the other would be at hand. We experimented by communicating with hand signals and waving our arms to find out what could be easily seen. This was challenging as both arms are needed for sailing the boat.

We had sailed for well over two hours without rest breaks. Although we did not make it to Milanda Beach we learnt today it was well within our reach. As we packed away the Toppers at the end of the day I felt exhilarated. Although exhausted I was bursting with excitement and the thrill of anticipation. My delight in sailing sometimes felt like a multi stretched piece of elastic. It stretched and expanded in new dimensions each time I sailed. How long before the elastic snapped back? At what point would it reached its limit?

On The Rocks!

Sunday 30th September

I have developed the habit of listening daily to the coastal waters forecast. Today's forecast said the sea state would be slight and winds SW Force 2 to 3. Perfect! We decided to give our sail to Melanda Beach a try.

Aware we had only just started our preparation program, we decided to give ourselves escape routes. We drove Sam's car with the boat trailer over to Melanda Beach in this morning. We may not need it, but it was there just in case we had problems or were too tired to sail back.

Pre sail, we reached an accord that if the conditions became too challenging before we reached the buoy we could turn back. We agreed that once beyond the buoy we would continue the sail to Melanda Beach. From there we could always tow the boats home on the trailer.

Sam led the way, sailing on a ***close reach***, with the sail pulled in tightly but not as tightly as close haul, (close to the wind but not the closest point of sail) at maximize speed but with greater control. He headed towards the yellow buoy. I managed at one point to catch him up and sail beside him. It felt great! It truly was a fantastic achievement for me. Sam recognized it as he gave me a broad grin and a wave of encouragement.

I felt every cell in my body fizzing with excitement as we approached the yellow buoy, sailed around it and kept on sailing. In the distance I could see Melanda Bay. As we sailed on it grew clearer and clearer. The bay opened out revealing the colourful fishing boats bobbing about in the cove. To the right was a clearly marked boat lane. This threw me a little, as I could see swimmers on both side of the lane I knew I must keep within its boundaries. As we tacked for our final approach the wind changed and within minutes I was hurtling headlong toward the beach. In panic I could only remember that to slow down I needed to turn out of the wind, but this would take me out of the boat lane. Then, with the beach rapidly approaching, I remembered: the sail is the engine, loosen the sail. I did. I immediately slowed down.

I hastily pulled up the dagger board and the rudder so as not to damage them on the shingle. I then leapt out of the boat, but I was a little too early. Still grasping the mainsheet, I held on fast as I went underwater. Greatly relieved to have made it close to shore at least, I swam her in the last few yards.

As I did so, I watched Sam beach his Topper perfectly. As we hauled the boats up, onto the shale beach beyond the watermark clearly visible because of the flotsam and jetsam, I felt grateful that I had already started my exercise program. Hauling the boat took a great deal of strength. I knew that already I was doing a better job than perhaps a few weeks ago. However, I wished I had started it sooner. As I dug my heels in, it had been quite a struggle, using the painter at the bow, to pull her up onto the shale beach.

Relieved to reach our goal we feasted on fish and chips, washed down by a celebratory beer at the Melanda Beach Taverna. With the sweet smell of success and knowing the sea state was good for our return journey, it tasted marvelous. Sam was delighted that we had made it so far. He was greatly amused by my dunking as I made it to shore and asked me if I had enjoyed my swim. We discussed our return sail. Sam suggested that in order to clear the headland and be free of the rocks and wind-shadow we needed to head straight out to sea. From there we would have to tack back and forth as we zigzagged our way home.

Rested and ready for the homeward sail, I launched Vitamin C off the beach. Once on board, whilst holding onto the rudder extension I struggled with the mainsheet. She was unresponsive and impossible to maneuver. When launching I had allowed too much slack mainsheet to trail in the water. The excess mainsheet was now wrapped around the rudder. Heading the boat *into wind* I quickly leaned right out to untangle it.

Meanwhile, the winds had quickly picked up, gusting to a Force 3 to 4. The sea state began to change. Small white horses began to form as I rounded the corner from Melanda Bay. I was already too close to the shore and rocks. The wind direction shifted again, this time by 180 degrees. The gusting wind caught my sail and the whole boat swung around. Horrified, I could see I was heading directly into the rocks. I felt helpless. The boat was moving backward, closer and closer to the rocks. I was rapidly being drawn onto the rocks by the sucking undercurrent of the barely visible sea caves.

I must turn her! Frantically I began using the pull on the sail and the pull on the rudder to gain control, even though I was reversing. Immediately I followed on with the push of the sail and push on the rudder to bring her back into the wind. Hopefully I could then sail out of danger on close haul.

However, I was too close to the rocks. I was in a wind shadow with no sail power. I could feel my panic rising. I was reversing her closer and closer into the rocks. I could not turn her into the wind!

Sam had sailed back to try and find me. He was watching on with horror, praying I could catch the wind and sail. Realizing my danger and distress Sam beached his Topper. He swam round the rocks to push me round and then swim me away to safety, away from the wind shadow. Half on and half off the jagged rocks, he gave the boat a great push. He succeeded! Neck deep in rocks and foaming water he was battling to stay afloat. He frantically waved at me shouting, "Go! Go! Go!"

The sea was building. As I looked back I could see the white tops of the waves thrashing against the rocks. Sam having swum out to get me away from the rocks was having difficulties battling through the churning sea. The undertow, which had caught my boat, seemed to have him in its grasp. It was strong and persistent.

I was transfixed. Torn by Sam's determination for me to head out to sea, I desperately wanted to go back and help him. I could see his Topper. It was still. The only movement on the beach was Sam's sail flapping despondently, abandoned. No Sam.

Suddenly I glimpsed a fishing boat, just by the rocks. They had been watching us. They could clearly see Sam in the water. Thankfully, they were *standing off*, waiting in safety, just in case help was needed.

With great relief I saw Sam's Topper mast wobble and begin bobbing around. She was on the water! Sam had begun to launch her. He was safe! I waited as I lye-to. I wanted to make sure he was up and ready to sail back. He signaled to me that he was eager to get going. I breathed a sigh of relief. I felt miserable that I had put him into that situation. He must be exhausted. It must have been quite a battle to get away from the rocks and back to the beach. It certainly would have been for me and I am a very strong swimmer.

Sam had overcome a longstanding fear of water and has been swimming regularly over the last month. I am thankful for that.

We had to sail through turbulent seas and building winds to get back into Pissouri Bay. Once again we experienced the waves being high enough for the boat ahead to completely disappear into the trough, before re-emerging. As the Topper mast is just under five meters this was a clear indication that we were sailing our little boats in waves of well over three metres plus. We knew we were testing the Toppers and ourselves to the maximum in these extreme conditions. I felt exhausted physically and emotionally, yet I knew I had to hang on. Vitamin C creaked and groaned with the effort she was making. The roller coaster motion of the Topper cresting and dipping into the wave was thrilling. Every now and again I saw Sam's boat pop up from the trough I was about to descend into. The adrenalin swooshed through my veins. No longer tired I felt ebullient and invigorated.

With Pissouri in sight we were back in the hubbub of jet skis, paragliding, bobbing canoes and catamarans. We had returned from a different world, world of basic survival. Every cell in my body fizzed. I had been exposed to life threatening danger and felt thankful for it. I had lived through moments of timelessness during the battle with the elements.

Sam was greatly relieved that we had made it back safely. I was mortified that my carelessness with the main sheet had led to my being forced toward the rocks. I had put him in danger. I felt indebted to him for coming to my rescue and told him so. He laughed and said. "Welcome to sailing". I had enjoyed the thrill and adventure, now I recognize sailing can be dangerous, very dangerous.

During our debrief Sam emphasized the importance of team work. It is vital to feel confident and trust when we are sailing longer distances in the catamarans that if one tires on the helm, the other can take over. If one crew member falls overboard, the other has to be able to sail the boat sufficiently well to rescue the other. When sailing in the Toppers, with the other Topper nearby, we each get a different perspective to the sailing position of the other boat. *Standing off*, away from the other boat you are better able to assess the bigger picture. We had a perfect example today, for as Sam was sailing ahead of me his focus was on us both reaching our destination safely. With nothing ahead of him to give proportion to the size of the waves, he was unaware that his boat was completely disappearing from my view, that the trough of the waves was so deep. For me it had been an adventure of survival.

As we packed away the boats, I dreamed of the warm bath waiting for me to sooth my aching muscles. I felt totally changed, reborn.

Playing Wind Tag

Tuesday 2nd October

We decided to sail the Hobie Wave, Kitty Moran, to Melanda Beach today. The weather report indicated the sea conditions would be ideal: a South Westerly Force 2 to 3 with soft seas.

The Wave is a very different boat to a Topper. With two hulls connected by the trampoline she is bigger. Being almost as wide as she is long, she is heavy. As such she requires much more wind to maneuver than the Toppers, which are light and flighty, more like arrows. However, when the wind and calm sea conditions are in her favour, Kitty Moran flies. Hobie Waves are stable, safety first boats, difficult to capsize and built for fun which is why they are so popular with the Water Sports Centers.

The downside is that, if the wind drops, wherever we are, we face the problem of being marooned. We do not have a rescue boat ready to hand with an independent crew to tow us out of trouble. We could be left sitting out on the water for hours at the very best. If conditions changed at Melanda, we would have to take the chance and leave Kitty Moran abandoned on the beach. Being as heavy as she is it would be very difficult to pull her up onto the steep beach but almost impossible to put her onto a road trailer to bring her home.

We sailed out of Pissouri Bay in high spirits, ready for a relaxed, uncomplicated sail. It would be our first visit to Melanda Beach with the Wave. But our light-heartedness began to sink as we headed towards Melanda Beach. The skies had begun to darken. The clouds rapidly built. We were sailing directly towards the darkest of stormy skies, which although quite some distance away, looked sinister and daunting.

Storms in Cyprus can have a hurricane quality. I have witnessed "twisters', spinning holes of wind and water, in both Larnaca and Limassol, a number of times. The centre of a storm is known as the "eye of a storm". This is an area of low pressure within the storm center. Within the eye there is no wind to navigate the boat. Once the eye passes over, the winds pick up and can be devastating. At the edge of a storm, the sea and the winds can be at their worst, very unpredictable.

Needless to say we would never go out to sea in that type of extreme weather. If such conditions had been even predicted we would not have ventured forth.

I had been eagerly looking forward to having lunch at Kyrenia Beach Taverna. Kyrenia Beach is in the same bay as Melanda Beach. The long beach is broken up by a small headland creating another sweeping mini bay.

Instead we stood off, watching and waiting, hoping for a change in the weather conditions, ready to fly out of danger if we must. Finally Sam decided it was just not worth the risk, I felt both disappointed and relieved. The possible dangers of sailing in such conditions where no longer an abstract in a book, but sat there right before me. Safety must always come first.

Hungry, as it was well past lunch time, we sailed back towards Pissouri Bay. I was astonished that ahead of us the sky cleared to a lovely Mediterranean blue. The water sparkled with bright sunlight. This lured us beyond the bay around Cape Aspro. Our hunger forgotten we continued our sail.

The tall impressive cliff face stretches for miles along the coast. The wind and sea erosion had carved organ pipes but this time of gigantic proportions. Each one broad and sturdy, substantial and significant, as, reaching up to the heavens they sounded their silent tribute. Scattered along the coast, inaccessible from land because of the cliffs were sandy beaches, each with its private cove and crystal clear, turquoise waters. The only visitors, goats, recklessly teetered on the narrow goat tracks as they foraged for an elusive tasty morsel of grass.

This was the furthest we had sailed to the South West. Far in the distance we could see Petra Tou Romeou known by the tourists and locals alike as Aphrodite's Rock, one of Cyprus's most famous landmarks.

As we sailed Sam enthused about sailing to Timi one day. This would be at least four times as far from Pissouri Bay as the trip to Melanda. We would have to pass by Aphrodite's Rock. That whole stretch of coastline was scattered with "rocky dragon's teeth" and great upended slabs of rock demarcating a rocky ledge less than half a kilometer out to sea, clearly visible at low tide. The tidal range difference between high and low tide, is only about ½ metre, the rocks are barely visible just below the surface at high tide. It would be quite treacherous. It would take a great deal of planning. I would have to be a competent helm by that time. These jagged rocks could seriously damage the hulls.

Unexpectedly, although we could see wind on the water ahead of us, the wind dropped around us. The giant cliffs had created an enormous wind barrier, a wind shadow affecting us even though we were quite some distance away from the shoreline. We floated towards the windy sections ahead of us, filled our sails with wind once more, came about and sailed further out. Sam handed me the helm. "Go and play", he said. I tacked then gybed, moving closer to the cliffs to find the wind shadow and then, just before, turned and sailed back out to sea, preempting and playing with this intriguing phenomena.

I loved this game. I was flirting with the magnificent cliffs and their wind stopping power. I felt more of a detective than a sailor observing the nuances and patterns of the water ripples evident through the changes and direction of flow, in order to unravel the mysteries of the wind in this magical place. Each time as I came about, ready to meet the clearly defined rippling margin, which was determined to separate me from the wind, I endeavored to increase my reaction speed, so that just before the first flicker of wind change I could turn.

Eventually hunger got the better of us. As we sailed back into Pissouri Bay we were followed by the golden hues of the sun casting its opulent glow on the sea behind us.

What an incredible day! Within a four hour sail I had truly experienced the fickleness of the weather, the sea and the winds. With Sam, I had sensed the danger which can occur if you choose to ignore the evidence of unpredicted oncoming storms. Later, during our debrief Sam emphasized that forecasts are a guide which can be very helpful. However, the weather you see before you is always right, forecasts can be dangerous.

It is vital to fine tune all our senses. Today I was more aware than ever before of the touch of the wind on my face. You can simulate it with stroking paint brushes of different sizes, qualities and textures across your face. With your eyes closed you can begin to recognize both the quality and the direction. A simple shift of position, by turning the head slightly so that the brush /wind touches a different point can radically change the information. Watching not only the flow of the water but also the way the wind plays with it is vital in calm waters. Catching the merest whisper of wind in a small dinghy can make the difference between reaching your destination or being stuck out at sea. I have observed that when the calm water changes to choppy, spiky peaks a gust of wind is about to come. The water appears to change before the wind actually arrives. Fascinating!

Transformation

Thursday 4th October

This week Sam has repeatedly suggested I take a Topper or the Wave out on my own. I have been reluctant to do so. He then relented and joined me, whilst at the same time making it clear that he had other things to do. I realize that encouraging me to sail solo is a great compliment, yet I feel that he is pushing me away. As sailing is becoming more and more important to me it seems to be becoming less so for him. Why? I am angry and confused.

I love the companionship of sailing together. Sam's sailing skills are a benchmark for me to aspire to. This makes it so delightful for me when I get things right. The motivation to get the boats on the water for our last few excursions has been driven by my growing passion for sailing. Even though Sam had come along, not wanting to disappoint me, frankly he appears to have lost interest and enthusiasm. He is distracted. His mind seems to be elsewhere. Maybe he is worried about something. I feel uncertain and afraid to ask him.

Destination sailing has really stirred within me an enthusiasm for sailing. I am hungry for it. I want to sail for longer, cover greater distances, discover some of the inaccessible places as well as sail to beach taverns. In addition to skill building, sailing is a creative, almost spiritual experience. It stirs something inside me previously untapped. Sailing is no longer holding me in a grip of terror. For me now, it is about sharing, laughing, planning and daring to do something most other people would not dream of and feeling proud of that. I love sharing this with Sam.

My progress is tangible. My rib pain, having raised its head to maximum velocity has now disappeared altogether. Physically I am different, more "cat-like" as I move about on the catamaran and much more confident in the more restricted space of the Toppers.

This transformation has expanded my confidence and seeped into every aspect of my life. My sense of self, alongside my balance and poise has blossomed. Even though it is years since I have worn high heeled shoes, I now really enjoy wearing them when I go out in the evening. Walking in them accentuates the fluid sense of full body movement that I am accessing on the boats. I used to prefer the safety and comfort of flat foot-shaped and frankly boring shoes. Now I am enjoying walking on the wild side!

Having heard people talk of the rolling gait of sailors, I am beginning to understand that more clearly. It is best described as a greater sense of ebb and flow and it feels wonderful.

No sailing for the next week as Sam is busy. It is time to delve further into the RYA sailing books and watch some sailing videos.

Heavens Gateway

Thursday 11th October

There has been no sailing for the last 8 days.

Yesterday evening Sam explained that he needed to spend dedicated time working on Triton, his 56ft motor sailor, moored in Larnaca Marina. He told me he has been busy over the last few weeks house hunting. He has found a small house with a garage and yards in the front and back of the house to store all the sailing gear. Sam is moving to Larnaca!

Today I feel numb, disconnected from reality as we prepare to launch the Wave.

We set sail at 4.30pm. Listlessly I helmed as we sailed and tacked cross the bay a few times and then Sam took over. No longer occupied I sat trying to think of something to say, feeling an enormous knot in my stomach tightening as the silence continued. We sailed out to sea, much further than we had done before. The air was perfectly warm with a faint brush of cooling humidity which feels soft on the skin. It is a glorious evening for sailing yet it all feels surreal. Sam continues, instructing me as we sail, as if nothing has changed.

As we sail further out, the coast line of the bay disappears to a dot. Within moments the sea-state changed. We are now sailing in what I can only describe as mature waves. They are bigger than the waves we have met before in every way but most significantly in breadth. Instead of the Hobie Wave being jolted over sharp, steep, capped waves, we are sailing with a flowing motion across larger, rounder more powerful ones. The wave height is about 2 metres similar to the height of waves we have encountered before yet the journey is qualitatively different. I feel lulled by the rolling motion. Sam notices and warns me that these are dangerous seas.

Sam hands me the helm, instructing me to watch out for the excessive dipping of the hull into the waves. If the bow is buried and held fast by the water, the boat will cartwheel, as momentum must continue, taking the heavy catamaran up and over. Even through my numbness I can see and now feel how easily this can occur in these waters.

My years of canoeing spring to my aid to help me to read the waves. I shrug off my sadness and shift into an intuitive autopilot mode, continuously watching and adjusting the rudder to send the bow across the waves rather than down into the troughs. This takes enormous concentration. In these seas, each wave is a potential, dangerous capsize yet the waves keep on rolling relentlessly.

As I make the final run home the darkening blue sky is smudged with soft brush strokes of dramatic pinks and purples as the sun starts to go down behind the Cape. We are carried by enormous undulating waves as we begin the journey back to shore. The wave movement, a continuous flow, is soothing and somehow comforting. The sea begins to mirror the sky. The soft sea blue is absorbed by the rose pinks, heliotrope and purples then finally shimmering, silky mauve. It seems as if we too have merged into the magnificent seascape. Sitting close to each other, deeply touched by the gorgeous display and the extraordinary raising and falling motion of the sea, we sigh in unison. It is heavenly!

A Fabulous Sail!

Saturday 13th October

With a Force 2 from the South we sailed the Toppers across the bay, heading North East in the direction of Melanda Beach. The sea was extraordinarily beautiful, soft, and almost mirror-like. Sailing beyond Black Rock, we sail the Toppers side by side and once we are around the headland, we shifted to broad reach with the sails out at 40° angle to the boat.

As I looked across towards Sam I could see him lounging across his boat, super cool, with his feet dangling over the edge, the tiller tucked under his arm with his mainsheet wrapped around his hand. With a smile, I remembered to bring Vitamin C's dagger board partly up, then tweaked my rudder up a notch thus creating less resistance in the water and positioned myself in the centre of the boat to maximize performance. I could see out of the corner of my eye, that this had certainly grasped Sam's attention. He suddenly shifted from his lounging position to sit upright, as I sailed smoothly past him with my sail billowing out. I felt myself expand with the sheer pleasure of the moment; I sailed on carving a perfectly straight line in the water.

Sam was laughing as he caught up with me. "Where did you get that trick from" he called across to me.

"I've picked up a few tips from the RYA books I have been studying", I teased with a grin. I was delighted when I spotted that he had made the same adjustments to catch up with me.

Sailing in tandem once more with the gently blowing southerly winds keeping us firmly on course it was wonderful to sit back and enjoy the scenery. We chatted across the boats, pointing out to each other the lovely patterns on the rocks above us, the variations of rose coloured striations which swirled and curled their way as they flowed, showing off the different layers of sedimentary rock as we sailed along the dramatic shoreline.

I pointed out two backpackers. I could see them gingerly picking their way along the pebbly path along the foot of the cliffs. This could only be done at low tide, creating a delicate time line. Innocent walkers would loiter at their own peril. Sam called out to me that shortly we would be passing above the spot where I had once had problems with the subterranean sea caves sucking me in towards the rocky headland. We would be giving that spot a wide berth. I was thankful for that. I smiled to myself knowing I had developed enough skills to do so.

On our previous voyages we had sailed out to sea towards the yellow buoy, which I could see bobbing away in the distance. From there we head directly in to Melanda Bay. Our route change today was due to the shift in the prevailing winds.

Once beyond the headland Sam sailed ahead of me. Suddenly, I saw Sam's sail swing violently 120 degrees. I saw him slip down into the centre of the boat. He completely disappeared! With the boom swinging round with such velocity it is vital to move out of the way fast. Otherwise, although fairly light, the boom driven by wind speed can inflict a mighty bang on the head. With the boat then unbalance a capsize can easily occur. Next moment his head popped up. He gave me a wave. He was OK! By sliding down the boat he had kept out of the way of the boom and kept his weight well distributed to maintain balance. Whilst preparing to gybe, necessary in order to turn the boat towards Melanda Beach, a sudden gust of wind must have taken him completely by surprise. This indicated there must be a major wind shift at that point. Pre-warned, I prepared and hauled the sail in tightly and also pulled on the kicking strap. With the mast and boom creating a right angle the kicking strap is the hypotenuse of that triangle. It is cleated on the boom to be easily loosened or tightened with a tug to allow greater or lesser movement of the boom. Whilst on the broad reach I had loosened the kicking strap to allow the sail to swing out. Now I needed it pulled in tightly to prevent the sail from swinging round violently.

I felt a knot of anxiety as I approached the point. I slid down into the centre of the boat and balanced on my trembling knees, aptly in the prayer position, ready to move in any direction. Cautiously I approached and gripped the mainsheet tightly. Suddenly the wind slammed into the boat spinning it. The sail span violently round. I only just ducked in time! I ended up lying in the bottom of the boat dizzy and dazed. It had all happened so fast! My prayers had been answered. I was really thankful not to have capsized into the autumn cooled water. I had managed to keep the boat upright and I was all in one piece. Wonderful! Still feeling dizzy and a little disorientated I was even more relieved that Vitamin C was now facing towards Melanda Beach. Recovered, Sam had to lye-to and had watched me at a safe distance. I sailed on to join him. He greeted me with a grin saying, "That was doubly unexpected. You seem to have been hit with an even greater gust of wind than me. Well done!"

As we jubilantly approached the beach and landed the Toppers we were greeted with smiles and open curiosity by the sunbathers on the beach, some of whom came over to chat. We certainly must have been very noticeable out there spinning around like tops.

Melanda Beach is an out of the way spot, you cannot really stumble upon it. Shallow waters offer a safe swimming area, wonderful for less confident swimmers. It attracts people who are looking for something a little different. The fish taverna itself, nestled into the cove, serves simple, fresh delicious food. It is beautifully situated overlooking the bay, peppered with brightly coloured fishing boats bobbing on their sea anchors resplendent with their rainbow colour baskets. A steady stream of smaller fishing boats pull up to the rickety jetty, their baskets filled with the Catch of the Day disappear into the tavern's kitchen, guaranteeing fresh fish.

We have another delicious lunch of fish and chips washed down by a beer. As we basked in the sunshine we laughed about the swirling rogue gust of wind that had caught us both out. Sam explained that it was created by the headland dropping sharply into a bay colliding with the wind funneled down the valley behind Melanda Beach creating a wind T junction.

As we launched the Toppers, we prepared for the punching, wind swirling phenomena. Sure enough, it was ready to try and catch us out. I felt the jolt like a sledgehammer as the wind punched and grabbed the sail. Following Sam's lead, I held on to the mainsheet and used the wind power to turn the boat, almost through a right angle. Perfect! I had a momentary glimmer of the elation knights of old must have felt when they tamed the dragon. The wind power would always be there but I could manage it and even work with it. I felt my whole self expand, filled with a sense of achievement and deep gratitude that I had the courage to keep on sailing.

As the wind had turned the boat into the direction I wanted to sail in, I followed the line of the cliffs once more, catching up with Sam every now and again. With the winds in our favour still, on a broad reach we sailed gently home

Looking back I realize it is quite some time since I have capsized my Topper. A few months ago this was a regular occurrence. For weeks I had been black and blue from bruising. Was I becoming a better sailor or had we shifted into some sort of seasonal wind change? Only time would tell.

Today's sail was so different from all the previous ones. I felt a deep personal sense of satisfaction. Having met the 'Wind Dragon of Melanda' and survived, I feel as if I have moved forward a notch. Sam does not shower praise, it is not his way, therefore today's' grin of appreciation meant a lot. However, I am not as dependent on Sam's approval as I was. I am building a deeper knowledge of myself. I feel a glow of pleasure that I can value my own courage and tenacity. I am no longer afraid of being afraid and making a fool of myself. Fear is an obstacle that we can move through. By doing so, once we are beyond it, looking back from the other side, we should value, even celebrate our own bravery and resilience.

Mystery Solved

Today Sam took me to look at his future home. It is situated in a quiet suburb on the outskirts of Larnaca. Larnaca is about one hour and fifteen minutes from Pissouri. An easy 100km drive on the highway. The house is in an area called Forest Beach, so named as it is close to one of the few remaining beachside eucalyptus forests on the island.

The house does not have the spectacular sea view that his apartment in Pissouri has, rather than facing the beach, the road runs at right angles to the busy main beach road. But it is only a five minute walk to the beach. As the outgoing tenants were still living there, we could only walk around and look from the outside.

My heart missed a beat as Sam pointed out the garage and potential storage space front and back for the Toppers and sailing gear and even storage for the Wave. Was this to be the end of my sailing? I tried hard to show some enthusiasm as Sam listed the benefits of its location. I had to agree it offered easy access to the sea for sailing. Already Sam had found a place for the Hobie 15. She was to be kept at Anemos Water Sports, which serves the hotel guests at the Palm Beach Hotel. She could either be stored in the boat park off the beach or sit on the sandy waterfront along with the rental catamarans.

We made a day of it. We walked the long, expansive sandy beach and then had a light lunch at one of the beach side tavernas. Sam explained how much better the sailing would be in Larnaca Bay. It is a wide, deep, open bay, spanning approximately 20 km from Cape Pyla to Kitti. The winds are regulated by the low lying coast. There is nothing too high or significant to create the wind tunnels or the air turbulence that we get in Pissouri Bay and Melanda.

Before we left for Pissouri I was introduced to Sam's new landlord. It was at that moment that I realized that Sam's move to

Larnaca was definitely going to happen. I was going to have to get used to it. I would have to endeavor to make the most of our sailing time while Sam was in Pissouri. Although Sam believed that we could still sail together when he was in Larnaca, I know how things can change.

Strangely I felt much lighter when I got home. At least I understood why he had been so busy. He explained he had been dashing about for week's house hunting. He had been distracted, worried about Triton, his boat in Larnaca Marina. There was a lot of repair work still left to do in order to make her sea worthy. He felt that if he was in Larnaca he would make better progress.

Rocking and Rolling

Wednesday 17th October

It has been a week since we sailed. Sam has been busy preparing for his move.

Today the continuing soft seas offered us an ideal opportunity to get Madonna, the tender out. Setting up was much simpler with a foot pump on either side. This added an element of competition as with a great deal of laughter, we challenged each other to see who fully inflated their side first. I later discovered that the air seeps into the right and left chambers uniformly therefore Sam's declaration that he had been the winner was highly questionable.

Despite my fitness training the heavy, cumbersome outboard motor is still such an effort for the two of us to lift and carry. Thankfully, Sam takes the heavy engine section and I take the lighter, more awkward, propeller end. The outboard motor can only be carried out of the jeep to the tender when it is ready to be launched. Sam is quite firm that the motor should not be sitting on the gritty, pebbly, sandy beach. The accumulated debris would lead to malfunction. The outboard motor is attached directly to the bobbing tender by Sam, with me waist deep in the water holding the tender steady.

I took the helm for the journey to Melanda, smiling as I did so, remembering my terrors on our first trip on the tender. I remember how rigid I sat, holding the tiller trying to control the throttle. Now I control it smoothly but then my untrained jerky wrist movement had the motor accelerating sharply and the tender leaping forward every few meters, throwing us both about. Learning to operate the outboard took practice and patience. Once mastered it offers a pleasant change from sailing and an opportunity to be on the water even when there is no wind.

The conditions are idyllic. The sun shines gently as the harshness of the summer has gone. The wind just manages to stir the surface, a cooling breath creating gentle ripples on the mirror like surface.

We were welcomed at Melanda as regulars. Our delicious lunch was ready in a jiffy. We ate then motored back just as if we were commuters.

Tenders and little motor boats are quite common on Melanda Beach. It is a very popular fishing ground. The dark beds of seaweed swaying beneath us brush the underside of the boat as we motor around the headland. Divers and diving schools are attracted to this and other areas along this stretch of coastline which host a rich array of sea life. The tall cliffs are the nesting grounds for Eleonora's Falcons. Local legend says the first pair of falcons was brought over as a gift for Queen Eleanor of Aragon, the wife of King Peter 1 of Cyprus, in the fourteenth century. They are stunning to watch as they swoop and weave, playfully in groups of twelve or more across the headlands and over the sea calling the typical falcon *kek-kek-kek*. They look similar to the small slender peregrine falcon, with its long pointed wings, long tail and slim body.

Many weekend fishermen use the launching area on Melanda Beach to drive their 4 x 4"s with trailers on which sit motor boats, rubber sided ribs and inflatable boats like Madonna, Sam's tender. With the tender we come and go and hardly anyone on the beach notices us. We have a very different reception when we sail our little brightly coloured toppers. They always attract attention. They make people smile. The red, white and blue sails are eye catching and the bright blue and red plastic hulls must appear child sized. They certainly are fun to sail. It must come as a surprise when two adults, each well over 170cm tall clamber out of each boat.

Certain safety aspects of sailing apply to all boats whether motor driven or under sail. One of the most important is an understanding that a safe boat is one that has as much surface area as possible touching the water. Despite the forecast of gentle seas, the winds and sea state built on the way back. With choppy seas the bow must lift to mount the wave. As the front of the bow reaches the peak of the wave it is out of the water, at this point the wind can catch the bow and flip the boat over. Today, in these conditions Sam is helming. To balance the boat and keep her nose down Sam and I had to move further forward and then swiftly move back as she dives down. As we do not have an extension arm on the tiller Sam's movement forward is limited to how far his arm stretches, therefore to compensate I have to move even further forward. With the waves pouring up over the bow I soon become soaking wet. Thankfully the constant movement keeps me warm. Once over the crest of each wave I have to immediately move far back next to Sam, as we do not want her nose diving into the trough of the wave either. With a heavy motor at the back the wave rolling behind us can quickly fill her with water. A rubber tender is very unstable in stormy seas. Even with the floor panels the whole boat bends and twists with the water pressure. I am so thankful I have already found my sea legs. It is exactly the type of rolling sea that would make a delicate sailor seasick.

Sam kept shouting encouragement to me over the roaring of the motor and the lashing of the waves yet never once taking his eye off the vulnerable bow of the boat. I hung on grimly, soaked each time as she rocks up and rolls down with each in coming wave. I slip and slither along the gunnels to each new position balancing the boat. I can see how focused Sam is, working to keep her steady whilst keeping the motor running at an even steady pace so that we keep moving forward. The 30 minute journey to Melanda became a one and a half hour, bumpy, exhausting journey home.

It is frightening how quickly a still calm sea can become turbulent and then a dangerous rolling, menacing mass of water. The weather shifted so quickly that it was impossible to pick out the changes; they all seemed to happen at once. I wish I could have filmed the weather shift and then watched it in slow motion.

Sam's focus did not waver, he watched and steered and kept shouting encouragement. He got us both home safely. A lethal capsize was avoided and I learnt the importance of finely balancing a motor boat in the worst conditions I have experienced to date.

I have always greatly admired the courage of the crews and supported Life Boat organizations. Today I experienced a glimmer of the dangers they knowingly face on a regular basis.

New Frontiers

Sunday 21st October

I have used the term 'soft seas' as it is a term used for coastal weather forecasts. I had not realized what a sweeping statement it is until these last few weeks. The range of "soft" seas is enormous. They seem to range from glass-like stillness through ranges of colour and hues, viscosity, clarity, temperature, temperament and a heart wrenching mystical otherness.

The conditions today are gorgeous. There is a shimmering, glossy, almost oil like sheen on the water. Hues mix and merge from turquoise to Mediterranean blue with splashes of mauve which dance, gliding, moving, shifting and parting in shimmering iridescence. Surprisingly, even though the sea is soft there is enough wind to sail the catamaran.

We set sail to Melanda on a broad reach, as we had with the Toppers a few days before. It was breathtaking. We skimmed across the silken water. The only water movement was the twin trails in the wake we left behind. With the sail out fully the wind blew us gently and steadily to our destination. It was effortless. We were able to enjoy each other's company and the beauty of nature surrounding us. These were rare, peaceful, shared moments as usually we were too busy helming and crewing.

Lulled into a state of euphoria, as we reached the headland Sam turned Kitty Moran to enter Melanda Bay. Instantly the wind thumped at the sail and whipped it around with astonishing force. I ducked, just in time. Such a large force on a bigger sail would have given me more than a headache. Kitty Moran teetered for a moment then settled. The wind was almost the same velocity as with the Toppers. However, thankfully with a heavier boat, the effect was not quite so dramatic. It simply woke us up from our dream-like state.

We sailed beyond Melanda, across the bay to the Kyrenia Beach Tavern. Melanda is a fishing shelter, set up to cater for small fishing boats, whereas Kyrenia Beach is a large expansive sandy beach which attracts swimmers and sun bathers. Knowing it is such a popular beach, we had popped in a few days before by road and asked if we could beach the catamaran there while we had lunch. They were delighted. However, they had stressed we must not go into the swimming area. With an enormous sandy beach to land on this was no problem. We beached a little way from the tavern, well away from the swimming markers. Lunch was delicious particularly as we knew today we would enjoy an easy sail back. To date this was our longest journey and well worth celebrating.

We sailed back in peaceful companionship. The wind conditions were perfect, adding a whole new depth of meaning to the phrase "just coasting along".

As I sat on the deck I realized that I had learnt my sailing skills in most difficult seas. My first exposure to sailing last April was in conditions where many dinghy sailors probably would not consider going out. The conditions we were sailing in today, however, would encourage people to dust off their boats and sail. Strangely enough, if I had started at this point I probably would have given up. From the beginning it has been the challenge that has kept my interest. The challenge included overcoming so many of my fears and terrors. Even on the days when I have been utterly disappointed and I had felt I had made no progress whatsoever, Sam's encouragement had enabled me to see that I had.

My greatest breakthroughs have taken place when I have got something wrong and had to put it right as soon as possible. The best example was my struggles with holding my line of sail. I had assumed I kept doing it incorrectly. However, battling to get as close as possible to the wind in a Force 3 and to keep your boat there requires as much strength as determination. It had eventually dawned on me that I needed greater strength and from that time I began specific exercises. My determination was needed. My reward is to sail these glassy seas and think, "Wow! This is so easy!"

Dying Winds

Monday 22nd October

With a forecast of steady SW at Force 2 occasionally rising to Force 3 today it is a perfect day for Toppers.

The Toppers were soon rigged and on the water. We were ready for some fun! We challenged each other to a race to the end of the Cape. We sped out with both sails pulled in tight and both boats heeling over. This is a precarious sailing position but I was already used to perching on the sharp edge of the hull with my feet secured in the foot-straps. My main sheet was pulled in so tightly that I had to wrap it around my hand to maintain the tension. I adjusted the sail by moving my arm forwards and back. My fingers and then my palm began to tingle with numbness. The blood flow to my hand was restricted by the tightly wound mainsheet. Determined, I held on. I was flying along, when a kilometer out to sea, the wind suddenly dropped. I almost capsized, as with no wind, tension was released from the sail and the hull slapped down flat onto the water.

I knew of the phenomena created by a wind shadow from the Cape, but today we were out much further. I looked round for Sam. We were so far apart we could not communicate, so we each had to rely on our own resources.

So began my-self directed lesson on windless sailing. I let my sail right out as if on broad reach. I tried flapping the sail whilst holding the boom. My objective was to scoop up any wind or even to create some. Nothing!

I brought the rudder up a couple of notches so that it was at right angles to the boat and lay almost flat on the water. I then sat on the stern to submerge the rudder. Thinking of a badger's tail, I used the tiller to move the rudder from side to side, disturbing the water enough to create some boat movement. This created a little bit of breeze but hardly enough to be used by the sail. The action of the rudder created a little forward momentum. Progress was very, very slow. The windless sea became calmer and calmer, almost glass like.

There was an outside chance that Yannos from Columbia Water Sports might have taken a group out in his motor boat to Aphrodite's Rock. He would be happy to come to our aid. However, with the cooler weather we were at the very end of the tourist season. I knew it would be most unlikely.

I turned and looked out to where Sam sat, equally frustrated. He gave me a wave. He too was making little progress. Our patience and perseverance mixed with a sense of comradeship where the only things that got us home.

Today I added more things to my rapidly growing list of sailing challenges. You need to be happy with your own company. If I had been impatient, angry and frustrated, railing against the perfidious wind it would have been a disastrous day. The weather is not trying to harm me, its idiosyncrasies are not a personal affront but the many and variable conditions which have offered me masses of learning opportunities. When sailing with Sam I am not alone. I am able to share my frustrations and question, question, question. Sam is always happy to direct me to the RYA books which have a clear accessible body of knowledge and experience which I can draw upon. I have become more realistic and accepting of my own moments of frailty and fear. These drive me through the next learning curve. I learnt that thankfully a boat is designed to move. With some water knowledge and versatility you can encourage a boat to move, however slowly, even without wind. But you do need oodles of patience!

The Thrill of Perfection

Tuesday 23rd October

I helmed most of our sail today. The objective was for me to keep making figures of eight. This is a vital procedure for man over board rescue (MOB). If someone falls overboard you cannot immediately stop; remember boats do not have brakes. Even if you manage to lye-to or go into irons immediately, you will already be beyond the MOB.

You must never abandon the boat to swim to the MOB. By doing so you are abandoning what could be your only means of rescue. As the MOB may not be able to swim to you, you must sail past them and tack back. In a dinghy you would turn into a close reach so that the boat can be slowed and stopped when the windward shroud is next to the MOB who can then reach up and hold the boat, helm gives a quick flick of the tiller to windward to prevent the boat going through the wind and positions himself at the windward shroud to bring the MOB into the boat. For catamarans the objective is for the MOB to be rescued from between the two bows. This however is almost impossible with the Hobie 15 as the point on the bow crossbeam over which the MOB would be brought into the boat is the highest point. The stern is much more accessible. If you miss the MOB you must continue round again completing the figure eight and starting another one until you are close enough for the rescue.

A repetitive sailing exercise like this may appear to many people to be boring. However, it was giving me time on the water I needed to work out some of my navigation glitches. In order to sail in a figure of eight you have to move the boat through all the aspects of sailing repeatedly. I get a buzz from doing something over and over again, pushing myself to get it right. Once achieved, I love repeating the process enjoying the thrill of perfection each time.

In order to sail, whether crew or helm, you need to be able to recue anyone who goes overboard. MOB rescue is a requirement of the RYA Level 2 sailing course. It requires enough sailing skill and confidence to helm the boat and bring it close enough to the MOB and lye-to, to help them back on board. This has to be done quickly and efficiently whilst keeping and eye on the person bobbing about in the water. Most MOB rescue situations happen in rough stormy weather or as a result of some form of boat failure. During these stressful situations the rescue has to be performed quickly and efficiently whilst keeping an eye on the person bobbing about in the water. Having the opportunity to practise the sailing procedures on a calm peaceful day like today has been ideal.

Reflections

Sunday 28th October

Sam has been engrossed with packing and preparing to leave his apartment. He came along to sail the Toppers with me today to enjoy the sea breeze and watch me helm from a distance.

We had been told storms were brewing and that they would hit hard and heavy in the next few days. The window of opportunity for safely sailing boats as small as the Toppers was getting smaller and smaller. Winter weather was beginning to set in. One minute we can be sailing an easy Force 2 then suddenly the winds start gusting and spinning at Force 3 to Force 4. The opposite can happen like today where there were very light winds.

As I sailed Vitamin C effortlessly in towards the launching point for perhaps the last time, I felt sad. I reflected on the cycles of my sailing. I had been on such an extraordinary journey over these last 6 months. I had had to push through the disappointment and frustration in myself that led to painful bruising and injuries. These stumbling blocks are as significant as the tumbles we take when first learning to walk. They are necessary in order to achieve the necessary breakthrough. Along with my growing sailing confidence there had been born a certainty, a deep level of trust in myself. I knew that my injuries would heal and become less frequent, as my sailing skills grew. As a movement specialist I know I move much better, far more gracefully than I have ever done in the past. My innate grasp of balance and poise has moved to a higher level than I ever thought I would aspire to.

I had learnt that sailing is about dealing with the day to day and moment to moment challenges; in particular, learning to be truly spontaneous in life threatening situations. I have reached a point in my sailing journey where my personal shift is about more than sailing competence. Confidently helming a boat has helped me towards being the master of my ship in life, learning to steer and adapt to upcoming situations as I move forwards towards my destination.

Shifting Sands

Friday 9th November

Last night was very, very stormy. Even though Yannos has warned us of storms I had persuaded Sam to keep Kitty Moran, the Hobie Wave, on the beach, hoping that we would have the chance for a last sail. I have been working today in Limassol and have been deeply concerned about the catamaran all day. I prayed that Sam had been down to check on her.

On my way back from Limassol I drove down to Pissouri Beach. It was still very windy and cold. As I parked my car, for the first time ever I could see surf boarders in the bay. They were having a fantastic time as the giant rollers tore in. I battled my way through the vicious wind along the footpath to the catamaran. In the distance I could see Yanis had already moved his Hobie Waves up off the beach. He had lifted them right up onto the footpath. When he had warned us about the incoming storm, we had tied Kitty Moran to a tree on the footpath and some metal uprights close by.

As I approached I could hardly believe my eyes. The whole beach, to a depth of almost a meter, had been completely washed away! Kitty Moran's hull was sitting precariously balanced on narrow sand-bar about 14 cm wide with a metre drop on all sides. The sand bar was being washed away as I stood watching in horror. I phoned Sam. Time was of the essence. If she toppled off her sandbar pedestal, whichever way she fell, she would be seriously damaged.

Sam was there in minutes. He immediately focused on the problem. The easiest solution he said would be to create a sand ramp and pull her back into the sea then walk her along to the boat launch area. There we could dismantle her and put her directly on the trailer. However, time was running out. The sea was much too rough. If we walked her round she would have slammed into us. We would risk broken limbs at the very least.

Instead, inch by inch we managed to pull her towards the path, tilting her so that her twin hulls were resting on the beach wall and her stern now resting on what was left of the sandy beach, stabilizing her. We lashed her tightly to the tree using lots of ropes. The sand bar washed away even before we had finished. We had been just in time.

I was so relieved. I would have felt terrible if, after such a wonderful summer of sailing, the boat had been damaged because of my selfish need to keep on sailing. We had been warned about the storm but I had chosen not to listen. Kitty Moran could have been floating out to sea lost and abandoned or pounded by the rocks because of it.

Bye, Bye Kitty Moran!

Thursday 15th November

At last the wind has died down. We untied Kitty Moran from the tree and gently lowered her onto the remaining sand. We decided to honour our sailing adventures in her with a last sail in Pissouri Bay.

After the storm the cold wind was a gentle Force 2. In normal circumstances we would not have taken her out as she was only just moving. We set off in low spirits. Sam would be taking her to Larnaca, I may not have the opportunity to sail her again. An era was ending. Sailing at a funereal pace we took her out to the headland just before Cape Aspro. We then tacked slowly and deliberately and sailed her directly into what had been our Topper launching point. It was shallow enough and safe enough to beach her there. Once we pulled her up onto the beach we began to dismantle her.

First we had to drop her mast and wrap up all the fixings and stays. We then pulled out all the ropes which had laced the two decks together and those that fixed the deck to the bow and stern. We removed these in a fraction of the time that it took us to meticulously lace them all together months before. The decks were then slipped out of their runners leaving two isolated hulls. The rudders and stern bar were removed, followed by the bar at the bow. That was it. She was no longer a catamaran but a collection of parts. She was packed in pieces onto the trailer and carefully tied on. With difficulty I held back my tears.

At each stage I felt physical pain of loss. It was I that was being dismantled. I felt like a gutted, floundering fish, landlocked. No boats, no sailing and very soon no Sam.

Toppers, Wave and Sam Move to Larnaca

Friday 16th November

Sam is all prepared, packed and ready to move to Larnaca. Madonna, the tender with her motor and the Toppers are packed in the removal van along with Sam's household goods. Kitty Moran sat sad and dejected dismantled on the road trailer. I looked at her with total empathy.

Shortly Sam would tow the trailer to Larnaca with the Suzuki followed by the removal van. We said our goodbyes and Sam set off to his new life, to dedicate his time to his other venture, "Tritan".

Would I be continuing to sail with Sam?

Sam has already invited me to Larnaca once he has settled. He made me promise not to stop sailing. To encourage me, he offered to leave me one of the Toppers or even the Wave. I appreciated his gesture but at this point I have no desire to sail on my own. I still had much to learn. I want to expand my skills.

I had already explored other sailing options. I still had connections at the British Base and with some luck might be accepted to join their Sailing Club. There is also the Paphos International Sailing Club (PISC) just less than an hour's drive away. I had heard they were a really enthusiastic bunch who had their own training programs and were eager for new members.

Sam has taught me a lot. As well as having the opportunity to use his boats, he has given me his time, encouragement and sharp admonishments when he felt they were necessary. The adventures we have had and the trust that has developed between us is very precious to me. More precious than I can truly express.

Our time sailing together has always been about choices. Sam chose to take me on as a student with a view to me being his crew. I am sure he regretted it many times over but despite that he followed through. I chose to continue sailing even after my terrifying experience at Black Rock, looking back even as a strong swimmer, I could have drowned. I accept the initial capsizes and bruising as I floundered at the beginning and moved beyond that. I chose to continue even after my first solo sail in Kitty Moran where I had problems with the rudder and brought the catamaran in through the forbidden swimmers zone. Sam was convinced that day that I was hopeless, but I stuck up for myself and argued my case. I then strove to prove him wrong over the following months.

There was an interesting shift for me that day. I had achieved rather than failed. Something deep within me began to stir, a whole new sense of self-trust and self-belief. I began to see myself as someone who could and would sail well. I felt proud of my courage and tenacity. That certainly had had plenty of opportunities to be tested! I could have chosen to walk away but I didn't. Of that I am immensely proud.

This is not the end of my sailing!

Index of Sailing Terms

P

painter, 21
point of sail, 11, 15, 16, 31, 33, 58, 78, 94, 95, 100

R

RIB, 84
righted, 4, 24, 26, 35, 72, 87
rudders, 4
run, 45, 81, 95

S

sheets, 5

shrouds, 15
standing off, 102
stern, 4
stock, 23

T

tell tails, 19
trampoline deck, 4
trimming, 4, 85
turn turtle, 98
turning into the wind, 6

U

upwind, 16

SUGGESTIONS FOR FURTHER READING

www.cautionwater.com
www.sailingbeyond.com
RYA GO Sailing! - Claudia Myatt
RYA GO Sailing! Activity Book - Claudia Myatt
RYA Start Sailing: Beginner Handbook – Steve   Sleight
The Modern Beaufort Scale can be found on:
https://en.wikipedia.org/wiki/Beaufort_scale